THE IMPORTANCE
OF BEING CONSTANCE

The Importance
of Being Constance

Joyce Bentley

BEAUFORT BOOKS, INC.
New York

To my daughter, Jade,
who has also feasted
on pomegranates

Library of Congress Cataloging in Publication Data

Bentley, Joyce.
The importance of being Constance.

Bibliography: p.
1. Wilde, Constance, 1858-1898. 2. Wilde, Oscar, 1854-
1900—Biography—Marriage. 3. Wives—England—Biography.
4. Authors, Irish—19th century—Biography. I. Title.
PR5823.B43   1984   828'.809 [B]   84-11102
ISBN 0-8253-0248-X

Published in the United States by Beaufort Books, Inc., New York.

Printed in the U.S.A.   First American Edition

10 9 8 7 6 5 4 3 2 1

Contents

List of Illustrations

Acknowledgements

I wish to acknowledge and express my thanks and appreciation to the many authors of Wildeana who have allowed me to quote from their works. In particular, that eminent authority of Wilde, H. Montgomery Hyde who has been unstintingly helpful. Isolde Wratislaw and the Eighteen Nineties Society for use of her father's memoir. Terence de Vere White for his permission to quote from *Parents of Oscar Wilde*. Felix Hope-Nicholson for use of his grandmother's journal. A. P. Watt Ltd., for permission to quote from Robert Hichen's *Green Carnation*. My thanks especially to John Blacker, grandson of Carlos Blacker, for his valued assistance. Lastly I acknowledge the congenial co-operation of M. A. Wicks, the British Vice-Consul in Genoa for his enthusiastic research on my behalf. Other material has been assessed from newspapers, gossip columns and books of the period—some only remotely connected with the subject but all of which have conditioned my view.

This biography could not have been written without the help of the many librarians and archivists in the following institutions: foremost, the Law Library, the Monaco Embassy, the British Museum, the Public Record Office in Ireland, the Clark Memorial Library, California.

1

Family Connections

Oscar Wilde wrote a play in 1894 called *The Importance of Being Earnest*, and in 1960 Michael Mac Liammoir staged a one-man entertainment on Wilde and his work, called *The Importance of Being Oscar*. It seems only right and proper, then, to entitle this biography *The Importance of Being Constance*. Constance? The question will be asked, who on earth is she?

Her full maiden name was Constance Mary Lloyd, and on 29th May 1884 she married Oscar O'Flaherty Wills Wilde, who became the centre of a homosexual scandal—the crime of the decade—which shocked and rocked Victorian susceptibilities. Constance is important because she was at the hub of the furore, a victim of the vituperation— a woman at bay with the world at her throat. Yet we have heard very little about her—about the life she shared with Wilde; how she coped with hideous scandal when it eventually broke, and what happened to her afterwards. So hostile was public opinion against the Wildes that frightened relatives immediately destroyed all letters and documents bearing the name. Their actions have made things difficult for her husband's many biographers. Some, having taken their cue from Frank Harris, have dwelt on her alleged stupidity. She has been lightly dismissed as "poor Constance" and portrayed as a "dumb

Victorian beauty". The question has been posed, "But what did you think your husband was up to, Mrs Wilde?" Her education has been declared as "lacking", her grasp of literature "inefficient", her life "ineffectual".

How, then, did this beautiful woman, with wide interests, fascinating friends, her own type of humour, her inherent generosity, become branded with such a reputation? It seems, at times, that there was a 'Let's put down Constance' campaign! If anyone could be said to have had a raw deal from posterity, it was Constance. Was she, as some say, "history's fall girl", or was she the heroine of the *fin de siècle*?

Clearly, it is time for her to emerge from the wings and take her bow—a bow which is long overdue. It is time for vindication—to present the converse case. All the protagonists in the drama—Ross, Douglas, Queensberry, Wilde etc—have often walked across the stage of history and had their say. It is now Constance's turn.

Nobody can ever know the entire truth, but by collating and sifting through all the available material and by delving into the past and taking a look at Constance's interesting and eccentric ancestors and relatives, there are many clues and hints to build upon. For any biographer is merely trying to piece bits of a puzzle together to reconstruct a picture. *The Importance of Being Constance*, therefore, presents another face to the Wildean saga.

The ancestors on her father's side of the family, the Lloyds, were a colourful and lively bunch of folk who certainly left their mark on posterity. They came of northern stock and were tough and opportunist by nature, first making a name for themselves in the county of Cheshire, where Constance's great-grandfather, John Lloyd, was an articled clerk to a Major Holland Watson JP of Congleton. He was also an ensign in the Stockport Loyal Volunteers, a regiment which Holland Watson commanded.

John was an ambitious young man; he married the Major's sister, Mary, or Molly, as she was called, who lived in Swinton, Manchester. By the year 1817 he had risen in station to become the Town Clerk of Stockport. A further accolade was in store. The industrial unrest which followed Waterloo, and which in four years was to lead to the Peterloo Massacre and the Cato Street Conspiracy, began to erupt in Manchester with the march of the Blanketeers. Several thousand out-of-work weavers gathered on St Peter's Fields and, armed with a brown-paper petition wrapped about their wrists and a blanket in which to sleep rough, intended to march to London and present their grievances before the Prince Regent. It was an ill-advised scheme, and Constance's great-grandfather earned for himself the dubious distinction of apprehending the Blanketeers. The furthest point they reached was Macclesfield—John Lloyd saw they got no further—for, as Town Clerk and solicitor, he is reported to have acted "with great energy and promptitude in putting down the insurgents". For this service he was rewarded with an appointment to the 'Ancient office of Prothonotary of Chester and Flint', which meant he became registrar to the courts of these counties.

The Lloyds had, among their children, a second son who became Constance's beloved grandfather. He was born on 1st September 1798, at Loyalty Place, Churchgate, Stockport. They called him John Horatio after the national hero, Admiral Horatio Nelson, who had recently won the Battle of the Nile, to say nothing of Lady Hamilton's affections.

John Horatio attended the Stockport grammar school and had George Back, afterwards the famous admiral and explorer, for contemporary there. Young Lloyd was also a champion bell-ringer at the parish church and was referred to as a "respectable youth". After leaving school he took a BA at Queen's College, Oxford, in 1822, when he was placed in the first class of both classical and mathematical honours lists, and proceeded to MA two years later. In 1823 he was elected Fellow of Brasenose, remaining so until called to the Bar at the Inner Temple in 1826. He joined the North Wales and Chester circuit, on which he became a popular figure.

In 1825 he had married his first cousin, Caroline Holland Watson, who was the seventh daughter of the previously mentioned Major Holland Watson. Through this marriage Horatio connected himself with a family which thrust its branches deep into the counties of Lancashire and Cheshire and possessed a family tree going back to Edward the Confessor. One of the Holland Watson nieces was Mrs Gaskell, author of *Cranford*. Sir Henry Holland was, via the Wedgwood family, a cousin of Charles Darwin and became physician to six Prime Ministers and Queen Victoria; he married the daughter of Sidney Smith, the famous wit, and toured Moscow at the age of eighty-five. Another member of this illustrious family was Sir Thurston Holland, who became Secretary of State for the Colonies in 1895, and when his distant relative by marriage, Oscar Wilde, was sentenced to two years' hard labour, he was upped from baronet to

Viscount Knutsford. So much, then, for the family to which Constance's grandfather connected himself.

In the 1832 elections for the Reformed Parliament, Horatio, being a popular figure about town, a good speaker and something of a wit, went to the hustings, advocating advanced Liberal views, in an exciting contest that necessitated the bringing-in of the militia. He was criticized for coalescing with the Conservatives on the last day but explained, with great good humour, that if he had not have done so, he would not have got in at all! Soon after, Caroline and Horatio moved to London.

In appearance, Horatio was not tall, and he was likened in later years to Mr Pickwick, being round and fat and as jolly as his gout and bronchitis would allow. But, at thirty-one, what he lacked in height he made up for in brilliance and ambitious drive. His maiden speech in the House was against the Irish Coercion Bill, and after the dissolution of the first Reformed Parliament he did not seek re-election but concentrated instead on his chosen career. So successful was he that he and his family were able to live in fine style in a great, balconied, stuccoed house in Lancaster Gate, Hyde Park, London.

They had five children, two sons and three daughters. The girls were named Emily, Caroline and Louisa Mary; of the two boys, the younger died in infancy, but the elder, born in 1828 and named Horace, lived to become Constance's father. Horatio made many influential friends, one in particular being Lord Brougham, lawyer, publisher and Whig statesman, who defended Queen Caroline when she was charged in the House of Lords with adultery. It was Lloyd who piloted through the House, for Brougham, the first Criminal Law Amendment Act, abolishing capital punishment for many nominal offences.

By the time he was forty-three, Horatio's legal practice was a popular society affair; he apparently never retired until 2 a.m. and was up again at 6 a.m. Brougham held out hopes of Lloyd's taking the position of Solicitor-General on the promotion of Lord Denman; but his burning the candle at both ends resulted in a 'breakdown' of health which took the form of exposing himself in the Temple Gardens. Constance was told in her later years that "he ran naked in the Gardens, to the great consternation of strolling nursemaids." Whether he revealed little or all made no difference to the outcome; he could no longer be considered for an eminent position. It is to Frank

Harris, the literary con-man *par excellence*, that we owe this irrelevant piece of information. Were it not given credence by Robert Ross, who, in his Notes to Harris's book, states that the charge against 'Horatio' Lloyd was of a 'normal kind', the reference would be as suspect as some of Harris's other statements. The confusion arises from a similarity of names. Constance's father was called Horace. Otho Holland confirms that it was 'Horatio', his grandfather, who thus erred and strayed, and not 'Horace', his father. According to the Law Library, there was no charge in the form of a prosecution, for the Temple Gardens were private property, and there are degrees of morality. Moreover, Georgian attitudes still prevailed, for Queen Victoria had only recently come to the throne and had not yet turned the moral screw. There was no suggestion, nor is there evidence, of Lloyd's being dis-benched or dis-barred. He took the usual course of retiring from public life for a while. People have short memories, and other scandals would soon occupy their attention. Travel was considered—that, and time—as being the great healer, so, with teenaged son Horace, Horatio took himself off to Greece, where he fell in love with all things Greek—especially the Ionian Bank, of which he became a director.

About 1845 he and Horace returned to London, just in time to be in on the great railway boom. Horace was despatched, against his own inclination, to Caius College, Cambridge, while his father was straight away caught up in the fascinating financial development of the railway system. The Greek trip must have been most beneficial, for, through sheer brilliance of mind, he soared to become the best living authority of his day on the legalities of compensation. He introduced what became known as 'Lloyd's Bonds', which enabled railway companies for the first time, in the teeth of an Act of Parliament to the contrary, to borrow beyond their actual resources, at a time when railway development was being held up by the Act. Society immediately forgot his 'aberration' for he was mentioned in the best places and regarded as a legal genius, making £20,000 a year for several years running, as counsel for almost every railway in the UK. It was on his advice that a company was formed for the laying of the Atlantic cable in 1860.

If Constance's paternal relatives were a jolly bunch, her maternal evened things up by being rather strait-laced. Providence had placed them wisely on either side of the Irish Sea, the Atkinsons in Dublin, the Lloyds in London. Her maternal grandfather was Captain John

Atkinson of the 60th Rifles—the King's Royal Rifle Corps. As an Army Agent, he was a kind of business manager and banker, taking care of the business affairs of officers in their absence. Constance's relatives certainly liked keeping marriage within the family, for John Atkinson's mother had been, before her marriage, Judith Holland Watson, one of the previously mentioned Holland Watson girls and consequently the sister of Molly, the wife of the Prothonotary who had put down the Blanketeers.

Not much is known about John Atkinson except that he possessed a fiery temper, much wealth and the ability to father hordes of children in the grand Victorian manner. He married Mary Hare Hemphill, daughter of a distinguished family from County Tipperary in Ireland. Mary's mother was Barbara Hare Hemphill, a novelist, albeit a sporadic one. She wrote two novels, *Lionel Deerheart* in 1846 and *Freda: The Jangleur* in 1857. This latter ran into three volumes. Her youngest brother, Charles, became Serjeant-at-Arms at the Irish Bar and later MP for North Tyrone, having the distinction of being the only Irish Liberal in the House, and later still was created Baron Hemphill, by Campbell-Bannerman. Charles lived a few doors away from the Wildes' house in Merrion Square, Dublin, and was Constance's favourite uncle.

John Atkinson and his bride lived in grand Georgian style, as did their counterpart in London, at 1 Ely Place, Dublin. Their second daughter, Constance's mother, was born in 1833 and named Adelaide Barbara, after the then Queen, of course. There were other children. Lots of them. With a glorious confusion of names, a doubling-up of first and second names as though they could not be bothered to think up new ones. Apart from Adelaide, the girls were Ellena Mary, Selina Maria, Malvina Victoria and Maria (again) Plunket. The eldest son, Charles, was resident in Australia, whether from choice or in disgrace is not known—for only the black sheep were sent out to a colony which in the 1840s still smacked of transportation. Then there is a proliferation of family-tree names, such as the boy named Holland Watson Atkinson or another, Charles Hare James Hay Atkinson—after which to find a mere George is a relief.

When John Atkinson died, he left his wife and young brother-in-law, the sole guardians of his "infant children". The confusion of names, the clutch of infants and also a clause in his Will with reference to "my present wife", indicate that he could have been either a widower or a divorcé, with a growing or grown-up family, when he met and married Mary Hemphill, who was much younger. That John Atkinson's widow was an astute business woman is borne out by the fact of his leaving her his wealth and house and investments, "to leave in their respective states or to invest same in any security she may think fit".

2

Adele and Horace Lloyd

Constance's father, Horace, had come down from Caius with a BA degree but, having done little work, took no honours. He was admitted to Lincoln's Inn in April 1849, aged twenty, and to the Middle Temple when twenty-three, he was called to the Bar the same year. All he seems to have inherited from his father was not an outstanding appetite for work but a flair for anything mathematical. In personal appearance, too, he differed from his parent. He was over six feet in height, slim of build, with fine, violet-coloured eyes, brown hair and a low, gravelly tone to his voice, and he is described as "looking distinguished". In manner, he was at first cold toward strangers but, after perceiving the measure of the company, soon thawed to become a lively and charming companion. There was in Horace Lloyd's character a combination of the dreamer, the gifted wastrel, the sensitive, something of a young man who was forced into a mould against his will. Travelling and living with his father in Greece before going up to Cambridge may have had a liberating effect upon him, for he had soul enough to appreciate the 'new-fangled' Pre-Raphaelite art. He was a favourite of Lady Mount Temple, a cousin of the Irish family by marriage, whose house, Babbacombe Cliff, was the temple of Pre-Raphaelite art.

Horace put his mathematical flair to good use, not on the stock market but on the gaming tables. While waiting for briefs to roll in, he spent many happy hours in his chambers over hands of Double Dummy. One of his obituary notices reported coyly, "Mr. Lloyd was fond of a gamble and spent many vacations at Homberg and Baden-Baden." He was an expert at whist and billiards, having so remarkable a memory that he could tell the last card in each hand four out of five times. Society columns report him as playing billiards, principally at the White Hall Club, where he was popular and where his colleagues record that "he gave too large odds." At chess he was a strong amateur and again is reported as playing at Simpson's Divan in the days when such legal celebrities as Joseph Brown QC did not disdain to amuse themselves there, and where the famous Buckle would sit, for eight hours, hard at play and call it relaxation! That he succeeded in his profession was in some measure due to his father's help and advice. Not unexpectedly he was classed as a first-rate barrister of "good address and tact". His low-pitched voice was not of the calibre to harangue a jury, nor had he pretensions to eloquence, but, seeing that his practice consisted mainly of settling appeals, it did not matter. "The judges", it is reported, "listened to his arguments with great deference."

Two of Horatio Lloyd's daughters had already married. Caroline became Mrs Raikes, and Louisa Mary married the Honourable William Napier in 1854. Emily remained single, living with her father at Lancaster Gate, being his hostess when he entertained and managing the palatial residence and staff with competent ease.

Between dealing with appeals and dealing out the cards, Horace found time to cross the Irish Sea and court his cousin, Adelaide Barbara Atkinson, or Adele, as she was known. He is said to have proposed marriage while she was playing the Bechstein in the drawing-room of her parents' house in Ely Place. she being twenty-one and he twenty-seven, quite the fashionable age in those days.

Adele gives the impression of being a beautiful, crinolined young lady of considerable accomplishment, though in what it is not clear. She must have been attractive to arrest the attention of Horace, who was a most eligible bachelor and heir to the Lloyd fortune. Mixing in society circles as he did, surely he could have picked where he would. That he picked a cousin from the same branch of the family as did his father was not altogether a wise choice, because the Holland blood which ran in their veins—as in their parents' before them—was tainted with what the family called "the Holland temper". "They're like devils when roused," observed one of the relatives. Love has never taken any notice of obstacles, and even if the unwise choice had been pointed out, it made no difference. On 28th August 1855—four years incidentally after William Wilde married Jane Francesca Elgee at the same church—Horace and Adele were joined in Holy Matrimony at the parish church of St Peter in Dublin, according to the rites of the United Church of Ireland, and by licence. The witnesses were Florence, one of the Lloyd cousins, and John Atkinson, Adele's father. Horace then took his bride across the water to London, where he rented a house in Dorset Square.

The infamous temper may not have been evident before marriage, for Horace, being a carefree bachelor of means, would have little to irk his natural irritability. Adele, too, coming from a strict military household, where there was room for only one hearty temper, that of her father, would not have been allowed the indulgence herself.

No doubt the couple were blissfully happy at first, but when the honeymoon was over, the actual business of living together was not at all easy. There are several references to Horace's "volatile nature" and Adele's "vindictive tirades". So what went wrong? Was her attitude aggravated by her husband's gambling habits? Coming, as she did, from a strict military background, perhaps she had no patience with his sensitive nature. She could have suspected him of being unfaithful when his business took him away from home—perhaps he was!

And what of him? He was not robust in health. Could this have added to his natural irritability? And the voice, so low and attractively gravelly—could it have been indicative of the pulmonary disease of chest and throat which brought about his untimely end? It says much for his popularity that his practice did not suffer due to his many absences, for business poured in on his return. His vacations, as time went on, were spent at more exclusive resorts with more exclusive people, to culminate at Baden-Baden with the Prince of Wales's set. One can pose questions *ad infinitum*, but the truth is most likely to be that their inherited Holland temper rendered the cousins entirely incompatible.

But at the beginning things were not too bad. Horace had for some time been toying with the idea of adding the family name of Holland to his own, and the birth of their first child, a son, gave him the ideal opportunity. They were living at 3 Harewood Square at the time, and the boy, who was born in November 1856, was christened Otho

Holland Lloyd. Two years later, in 1858, the subject of this biography, Constance Mary Lloyd, was born.

If old Mr Lloyd hoped that marriage and fatherhood would settle his son, he was disappointed, for Adele's carping nature stood no chance against the long-standing fascination of the gaming tables, be they whist, chess or billiards. It is recorded that she often returned to Dublin to stay at Ely Place. The visits could have been 'going home to mother' in character or merely for company while Horace was out of town.

Temper-wise, there was not much hope for the children of this marriage. Otho in later life admitted to being "short in temper", and Constance, as some of her letters show, could be as vindictive as her mother, when provoked. With such a turbulent background it is not to be wondered at that, as she grew up, Constance's favourite relative, apart from her father, was the cheerful, Pickwick-like Grandpapa Lloyd.

When Constance was six, the family moved to 42 Sussex Gardens, in the parish of Paddington. The properties there consisted of handsome, three-storeyed houses, set well back from the street by long front gardens, and even in these days Sussex Gardens, when sampled on an early morning in spring, before the internal combustion engine is awake, is redolent of a more leisured and privileged society.

The Lloyd household employed six servants: a butler, two housemaids, a cook and a kitchen maid—a mere nothing compared to the staff at Ely Place and Lancaster Gate. Sussex Gardens was not far from Grandpapa Lloyd's house, which appeared to be the rallying-point for the family. Emily was at home, unmarried, and the other two sisters and numerous friends and relatives converged in true Victorian style. Over the tinkle of teacups and rustles of taffeta the conversation would turn to 'Horace's wife', who for some reason was not very popular.

Otho received his education at boarding-school, while Constance, it seems, received hers from tutors and governesses, at home. In the 1871 census all the family were present, with the exception of Otho, and Constance is described at thirteen as a "scholar". While Otho was away at school, his sister would not have been a lonely child in terms of company, for there were many cousins, and one especially became dear to her. This was Eliza, Aunt Mary Napier's daughter, who remained staunch and true until Constance's death. But death was a long way off in those childhood years of the 1860s.

3

Constance and the Pre-Raphaelites

When Constance was two years old, Grandfather Atkinson died, and as their Lloyd grandmother had been long gone, the children were familiar with only one grandparent from either side of the Irish Sea. John Horatio's mansion at 100 Lancaster Gate still exists. It has been for many years a hotel, but from the exterior little is changed, and it still retains its former splendour and prestige. Mrs Atkinson's residence in Ely Place is also carefully preserved as part of Dublin's Georgian heritage, a souvenir of a more elegant and gracious age.

It was this quarter of Dublin with which Constance was familiar. As a visitor to her grandmother's house, she and her many Irish cousins took part in the children's social whirl of birthday parties, garden parties, fêtes and fairs; there was the skating rink and dancing lessons, all attended by local children. The children of Sir William Wilde, who lived just around the corner from Ely Place, knew some of Constance's cousins and most likely knew Constance as well. Mrs Atkinson was on calling terms with Lady Wilde, and the former's younger brother lived only a few doors from the Wildes.

Mid-Victorian society in Dublin was both insular and provincial, a close society where everyone knew everyone else; it was the habit of all staunch Liberal families to worship at the fashionable church of St

Stephen's, and both the Wildes and Atkinsons were of the Liberal persuasion. From being quite young Constance was familiar with the sight of Sir William Wilde tearing about Dublin in his pony and trap. He was a small man, who looked anything but the famous ear and eye surgeon he was, still less the author, the authority on Celtic archaeology and a member of the Irish Academy. He had three children, Willie, the eldest, born in 1852, Oscar, who was two years younger, and a daughter, Isola, who was about the same age as Constance.

When married and with children of her own, Constance was quite happy to allow them the freedom of the house and to mix with the grown-ups in the drawing-room—a state of affairs which did not occur in her childhood. Had she then, through early association with the Wilde family, caught a glimpse of another world where it was not considered improper for children to mingle in the company of grown-ups?

If London did a roaring trade in scandals, Dublin was not far behind. In 1862 Sir William Wilde was accused by a half-mad woman, called Moll Travers, of rape. The ordeal for the Wilde family lasted two years and culminated in a trial, the newspaper coverage of which, in both London and Dublin, was delicate in the extreme and detailed in particular. All was faithfully, and salaciously, dwelt upon. The outcome was an acquittal for Sir William, but he had to pay the crippling costs, and although he was cleared, speculation was rife long after the trial was cold.

In this era when children were 'seen and not heard', when newspapers were kept out of reach, when questions about what was displayed on hoardings and placards, and what the newsboys were shouting, were fobbed off, adults often betrayed themselves. A knowing glance, a hushed reference and whispers only served to heighten the curiosity of young minds. It also impressed on them the importance of not being found out. The Irish cousins, those of an enquiring age, would be very much aware of the scandal which shook Dublin, and later it would consequently have come to Constance's ears. When it did, her sympathy would have been with the Wildes, for might there not have been whispers among the grown-ups about the vagaries and vacations of her own dear father? And among cousinly gossip even the gambol of Grandpapa Lloyd among the nursemaids, all those years ago, may have been discussed with smothered giggles. No wonder the fear of scandal was bred into Otho and Constance Lloyd, a fear which was to haunt them throughout life.

Reality was to be ignored at all costs. This was the unwritten dictum. And if anyone had the capacity to ignore reality, it was Lady Wilde, who, ignoring her husband's infidelities, and there were many, gestured expansively and said, "I soar above the miasmas of the commonplace." To the growing Constance, bound by the military precision with which Mrs Atkinson ruled her household, and the aloofness of her mother, the highly unorthodox and happy-go-lucky Wildes seem a fascinating lot. For, after all, their mother was 'Speranza', who had written under that name fiery and patriotic articles for the Irish nationalists. Further, she was a poetess and a translator; she wrote books, was tall, dark and strikingly theatrical and held a salon on which the literati all converged. Constance's mother did nothing and must have seemed colourless in comparison.

Then there were the Wilde boys, who, being in the same age group as the Irish cousins, occasionally moved in the same circle. They too were outgoing, affectionate creatures, which Constance's own brother, Otho, was not. Otho gives the impression of being something of a bear, a bit stuffy, although he proved to be a good, solid Victorian brother on whom she could always rely.

Three years after Sir William's ordeal, the Wildes were in the public eye again—not that they were ever really out of it—but for a totally different reason. Dublin lent its sympathy, as only Dublin can, when the blinds were drawn at the Merrion Square house. Isola had died of scarlet fever. She had been a merry little spinning-top of a girl, with waist-length golden hair, and her death devastated the Wilde family. She was buried not in the family vault but at Edgeworthstown, where they had taken her to stay with her uncle, the Reverend William Noble, at the Glebe, in the hope of the fresh air dispelling the fever. The Wildes had worshipped Isola; they had loved her extravagantly; and her favourite brother later preserved her memory in a poem:

REQUIESCAT

Tread lightly, she is near
under the snow,
Speak gently, she can hear
The daisies grow.

All her bright golden hair
tarnished with rust,
She that was young and fair
Fallen to dust.

> Lily-like, white as snow,
> She hardly knew
> She was a woman, so
> sweetly she grew.
>
> Coffin board, heavy stone,
> Lie on her breast,
> I vex my heart alone,
> She is at rest.
>
> Peace, Peace, she cannot hear
> Lyre or sonnet,
> All my life's buried here,
> Heap earth upon it.

Constance Lloyd emerged from childhood with all the graces of her father. She had inherited the violet colour of his eyes, a low, husky voice, slim build, thick brown hair and a quiet look of reserve. Otho resembled the Atkinsons, brown of eye, tending to stockiness and freckles, with a scholar's aptitude for shunning the social scene.

Constance adored her father, and what some called his 'wayward-ness' appeared to her to be 'bohemian'—his absences only served to heighten the romantic light in which a growing daughter often views her father. About this time in her life, she was packed off for some reason, at her father's instigation, to live for a while with a cousin by marriage, Georgiana, Lady Mount Temple. The reason was probably a clash of teenaged daughter and mother problems in which Constance would come off worse.

Lady Mount Temple lived at Babbacombe Cliff, two miles from Torquay and overlooking Torbay. The house was unique; it was designed by John Ruskin and decorated mainly by Burne-Jones and William Morris and was a veritable wonderland of Pre-Raphaelite art. If there was a special bond between Horace Lloyd and his daughter, it was more than likely to be the appreciation of this art which he passed on to her. Having been told stories of the marvellous décor by her father, there was no doubt that Constance would love it. Which she did.

A strong and affectionate bond developed between the impression-able young girl and the tall, stately Lady Mount Temple, whose husband had been the stepson of Lord Palmerston (he also had for his uncle Lord Melbourne, and on the death of both, Mount Temple became heir). In fact, Georgiana came to fill the place in Constance's heart which, for some reason, her own mother had never cared to claim, and she became the 'Mia Madre' referred to in Constance's later letters. Denied sympathy, affection and encouragement in her own home, she sought and found it in abundance at Babbacombe Cliff. Her ladyship was shrewd, witty, a widow with an immense fortune, and with her came the first of three life-long friendships which Constance struck with unconventional and spectacular women.

Lady Mount Temple's house has been a hotel for many years, and although the 'Mount Temple Inn' tacked onto the building would make John Ruskin turn in his grave, the rest of the lovely old house remains much as it was. The interior is still rather gracious and contains many original facets, one being a superb William Morris ceiling. About a mile away, on the promenade overlooking the bay, is a drinking-fountain erected by the local benefactress at the turn of the century. A small bronze statue of the elderly Lady Mount Temple graces the top of the fountain—eccentric to the last, with a parrot on her outstretched wrist.

It was while staying and travelling with the "Mount Temple ménage" that Constance's mind opened, like a flower to the sun, soaking up John Ruskin's thrilling concept of beauty, for this man with his crystalline eyes and a passion for Lake Windermere was the sole arbiter of art and culture. Those two words summed up the wonder of Babbacombe Cliff, and Constance Lloyd had gone among it, eager to embrace the doctrine of the Pre-Raphaelites. Young and impressionable, she took it all in, caring nothing for what Mama might think.

Had there not been this link, this interlude with Lady Mount Temple, it would have been impossible for Constance Lloyd to have held her own with Oscar Wilde. The Mount Temple ménage lifted her out of one environment to another. Already primed by glimpses of the unconventional Wilde family, and with the encouragement of her father, she approached the transition and absorbed every precept of Pre-Raphaelite art.

It was as part of this élite circle that her education was improved and extended; nurtured in such an atmosphere, it was not surprising that her taste in poetry ran to the Romantics, John Keats being uppermost and Dante a close second. She became knowledgeable on Tasso and Petrarch and, under the influence of William Morris, tackled all kinds of intricate embroidery and needlework.

Most Victorians were taught to play the piano as a matter of course, and Constance had been no exception, but while she was at Babba-combe Cliff, her concept of music—and heaven knows what else—was broadened by her meeting with the second spectacular woman in her life, Margaret de Windt, who in 1869 had married Sir Charles Johnston Brooke, the second Rajah of Sarawak, and so became the Ranee, Lady Brooke. She was a lively and unconventional creature and as such could not fail to capture Constance's imagination.

The Ranee's marriage had been undertaken by a sense of duty typical of the Victorian age. Charles Brooke was a rather bleak man who concealed every emotion and was a martinet of the first order. His romantic approach to women was phrased in French, and his habits were Spartan to the extent of sitting on hard, upright chairs. "Don't believe in fripperies," he would bark, "damned effeminate. Never relax and your stomach will stay where it should be; good for the organs to remain upright." He was twenty years older than Margaret and courted her in spite of being in love with her mother. He, like Constance's father, proposed marriage while she was playing the piano. Was it the romantic 'in thing' or merely an occupational hazard? However, frock-coated and top-hatted, Charles Brooke had, to the strains of a Chopin nocturne, made his proposal by stiffly placing on the eighteen-year-old Margaret's lap a piece of paper on which he had scribbled the following lines of doggerel:

> With humble demean if the King were to pray
> That you'd be his Queen, would not you say nay.

Margaret did not say nay. Her mother had arranged the match, and it seemed to her, at the time, something of an honour to be wooed by this frosty, unapproachable man.

Her adaptability in relating to the Borneo scene from the social gentility of English country life was nothing less than amazing. In the early days of her reign she had accompanied her husband on an upriver expedition as far as Simangang, where she awaited his return in the fort. Her brother, Harry de Windt, relates: "There was not even a piano to beguile the time, and the Ranee having read and re-read her stock of French and English literature set to work study-ing Arabic under the tutorship of a septuagenarian. The heat was too great to go out until the evening, when the lonely European lady and her aged escort would pace solemnly up and down the strip of road in front of the bazaar. A solitary dinner in the gloomy hall of the fort, amidst ghostly shadows and scuttling rats ended the day."

The Rajah had been absent for about a month, and, having heard a great commotion outside, she thought it was her husband arriving with his native warriors. Instead, it was a rebellious chieftain, who, knowing she was defenceless, demanded money. A shower of blows resounded from the gateway. "Let them enter," said the Ranee, ignoring the tears and protests of her serving-women. The doors were thrown open, and the chief—who was a noted head-hunter—swaggered in with a dozen or so followers. The sight was not a pretty one. Every man was armed to the teeth; their faces were tattooed; streaming black locks, protruding ears and great tiger tusks added a finishing touch. Tufts of hair, shorn from the dead, hung sporran-like from shield and spear. The chieftain told the Ranee he was going to join the Rajah and needed the money to finance the trip. "You have nothing whatever to do with the Rajah," she replied, "and I shall not give you one cent. My husband may return at any time, therefore be careful what you do. Besides, we have guns," she added pointing to some thirty-two-pounders and complacently ignoring the fact that there was no one to fire them. The words had scarcely escaped her lips when the distant sound of her husband's victorious return induced her to add, "And now, if you will take my advice you will escape without delay." After a mutinous pause they took advantage of her offer.

The first children of the marriage, two boys and a girl, died of cholera in Borneo and were buried at sea. Due to the Rajah's partiality for native women, Margaret eventually left him, but because an heir was needed, she dutifully returned, as though on a shopping expedition, for some more.

Charles, always generous in this respect, provided her with three sons, whom she wrapped up and brought to England, where, at her house, Grey Friars, in Wiltshire, whither Lady Mount Temple had despatched her entourage, Constance met her for the first time. A striking woman, there was nothing feminine about Margaret, or her country house. Her brow was low and her chin was long, but she had magnetic blue eyes which entranced all who met her, and a marvellous personality. She adored music and later in her life formed a women's orchestra. Estranged from the Rajah, she lived for her sons and her music—not to mention her passion for scarlet-winged macaws and the green parrot which often reclined on her wrist.

Keeping such company, it cannot be wondered at that Constance became an incurable romantic, a total convert to the Pre-Raphaelite view of life, and at seventeen she was a beautiful young girl.

This golden era came to an end with the death of her father on a Monday morning at the end of March 1874. It was quite unexpected and according to the physician was the result of "pulmonary disease of the lungs and throat" occurring after a short illness which could have been a bad dose of influenza. Horace was forty-six, and his death was a terrible grief to old Horatio, who was seventy-eight and plagued with ill health himself.

The funeral of Horace Lloyd QC was well attended, and the man whom some regarded more as a gifted wastrel than as a good QC was gloriously vindicated. He may very well have been 'wayward' and all the other things people said, but his funeral brought glowing orations not only from legal colleagues but from scientists and civil engineers—for what reason is not known; and the Prince of Wales's circle, at his death, did not forget him.

The funeral carriages, horses dressed overall in black ribbons, bore the party to Lancaster Gate, where the suave and capable butler, Henry Riches, had prepared refreshments.

Horace had made a will ten years after marriage leaving all his effects to "his dear wife Adelaide", but nine years later the effects did not amount to much. They were under £12,000 and insufficient to maintain his widow, educate his son, destined for Oxford, and provide a marriage settlement for his daughter. In a letter two years before his death Horace Lloyd had aired his views on card playing, deploring the fact that "the great fault of modern play was not finessing sufficiently". Finessing was an attempt by a player holding a higher card to take the trick with a lower, which meant of course risking a loss. Horace had evidently finessed too much. Adele left the house in Sussex Gardens and set up her own place in Devonshire Terrace, near Hyde Park, where she insisted her daughter live with her. Being under age, Constance could do nothing but comply and only watch with envious eyes her brother going off to university, financed, of course, by Grandpapa Lloyd.

4

Constance and Aestheticism

Adele's insistence that her daughter stay at Devonshire Terrace could have been an attempt to make the girl aware of what her beloved father's recklessness had brought them to. There was no money now to go wandering about the Continent with the Mount Temple ménage, not to mention the expense of clothes such trips entailed. It could have been an attempt to rescue her from this 'arty' way of looking at things, which the cold and practical would regard as suspect in the least. With inherent vindictiveness, the lack of a marriage settlement would have been flung at Constance's head, and the lack of money laid squarely at Horace's door. As Constance was in great demand for playing the piano at her mother's 'Afternoons', Adele could have been jealous of her expertise, even her looks. Whatever the cause of friction in that household, friction there was, and Constance, being endowed with the same brand of temper, would be inclined to give as good as she got.

Under the circumstances, any opportunity to go to Dublin out of her mother's way would surely have been seized. The spacious elegance of Hepplewhite and Chippendale which was Ely Place could not compare with the Pre-Raphaelite décor of Babbacombe Cliff, but it was better than the sepulchre of Devonshire Terrace. Constance was popular with her cousins and their friends, and joining in their activities must have seemed like heaven. Even the ice rink, where mamas and aunts sat at ornate tables to hatch out next season's brood of engagements, would have its attractions. Not the least being Lady Wilde, conspicuous in yellow silk and black lace. There was Willie, vivacious and handsome, but no Oscar—he was at Oxford.

Lady Wilde had written to Oscar, "Look up that brilliant Lloyd boy, you'll have a lot in common. . . ." But, Oscar did not look him up, and they, as yet, had nothing in common. According to Otho, he met Oscar at the Merrion Square house when his grandmama sent him to call on the Wildes. Later, in their first year at Oxford, they met out of doors, and Oscar invited him to call on him at Magdalen. Otho later intimated that he was in awe of Oscar's intellectual capacity.

Otho Lloyd was a very serious young man. He did not decorate his rooms with blue china or hunt for Japanese ware; he did not follow any crazes of the day but wore a moustache and side-whiskers, with the air of a man twice his age. He was a moderate lad, conventional and very much out of the Atkinson mould, given to irritable outbursts of temper and yet, to Constance, indispensable as a buffer between herself and her mother.

While in Dublin, Constance enquired after Sir William, who, suffering from the crippling costs of his court case and having never recovered from the death of Isola, was by now an ailing man, spending most of his time at Moytura, his country house on the shores of Lough Corrib.

It also appears that there was an offer of marriage while Constance was in Dublin. There is no clue to the quarter from which it came, only the comment of an Irish aunt who thought her a fool to turn it down—especially as she had no marriage settlement. Adele would no doubt have been surprised and endorsed the comment of the aunt. But Constance was firm; she had a mind of her own and was not being coerced into marriage with someone she did not love, as the Ranee had done, and many more besides.

If Constance was not in Dublin at the time of Sir William Wilde's death, the relatives would have written to tell of his burial with full honours, for Uncle Charles Hemphill was present in his Serjeant-at-Arms regalia. The funeral was lavish. The Chancellor, the Lord Lieutenant himself, all Dublin Castle, it seemed, turned out, as well as the Gogartys, the Guinnesses and the Home Rule League. There is no doubt that the Irish cousins followed the doings of the house of

Wilde with a quaint interest, and if Constance had not been interested, surely they would not have bothered to keep her informed? Lady Wilde, too, would not have troubled to mention Constance and her family in letters to Oscar if they had not known each other socially.

Back in London, visits to Lancaster Gate and outings with cousins must have made life a little more pleasant. Aunt Mary Napier was Constance's favourite aunt and took it upon herself to see that Constance's social life was not neglected. One such highlight to which all 'their set' were invited was a ball to which Oscar Wilde inveigled an invitation, via Gussy Cresswell. Cresswell, it seemed, wanted to meet Sarah Bernhardt, and Oscar promised to bring about an introduction if Gussy would, in turn, introduce him to some girls. Whether Constance and her cousins featured in this meeting of girls, or were present at the ball, is open to conjecture, but as she was a cousin by marriage of Laura Troubridge, who was also there, and as Aunt Mary Napier was also interested in the orphaned Troubridge girls, it is likely she was.

Oscar at this time was a fine young man, tall, well built, broad of shoulder. His heavily lidded eyes were blue; his hair was amber and modestly waved; his clothes were impeccable; and although he was still only an undergraduate at Oxford, he had developed a charm which made Laura Troubridge enter into her diary that she and her sister had met Oscar Wilde the poet and both had fallen "awfully" in love with him.

It has been said that Constance, when she was about nineteen, went to live with her grandfather, because of her mother's marriage to Charles Swinburne King, who held a minor position in the Foreign Office. It was more likely her mother's attitude toward her, which was considered bordering on hostile, that prompted Horatio to take his granddaughter to live with him at Lancaster Gate; this is borne out by the fact of Adele's not re-marrying until October 1878, and by then Constance was of age and could have left home without parental consent. Moreover, Adele married not 'Charles' but George Swinburne King, 'Gentleman', of Ealing—and according to the Foreign Office lists, he held no position there, minor or otherwise.

With the move to her grandfather's house, things began to look up again for the eighteen-year-old Constance. Her mind was set at rest regarding the embarrassment of a marriage settlement, and due to Lady Mount Temple's being a life-long friend of Horatio Lloyd, he was more than willing for his granddaughter to be taken under her ladyship's wing again, to be whisked off to Italy, where the Ranee was now resident.

Travelling on the Continent gave Constance the opportunity to become fluent in French and Italian, already being able to read and converse well in both languages. Some of the vacation was spent among the glittering society of Monaco, whither the Ranee had dispatched her entire house party as the mood dictated. It was here that Constance met the last in the trio of outstanding and remarkable women who influenced her life and remained her friends. Alice, the beautiful young widow of the French Duc de Richelieu, was grandniece of the poet Heinrich Heine and was later to become Her Serene Highness Princess Alice of Monaco. At the time of this first meeting, Alice was the golden-haired darling of Monegasque society, a great patron of the arts and theatre and, like her friend the Ranee, passionately fond of music.

If Constance had been, as is often stated, merely a "dumb beauty, pedestrian of nature, inarticulate and void of opinion", she would never have kept the friendship of Lady Mount Temple, the Ranee or the sparkling Alice throughout her life. Victorian society did not suffer fools gladly, and if Constance had nothing else to offer except her good looks, she would have been quickly shaken off like a poor relation, after the first visit.

In forming quite deep attachments to these women it is evident that the impressionable Miss Lloyd was attracted to the outré and eccentric—a taste perhaps started by glimpses of the Wildes in Dublin? Or rebellion against the constriction of her conventional up-bringing. Whatever the cause, the fascination was there. Regarding her looks, all her husband's biographers are unanimous in their confirmation of beauty. Pre-Raphaelite young ladies modelled themselves on their heroines, Janie Morris and Elizabeth Siddall, stretching the neck so it became long and graceful and practising a certain pursing of the lips. With her straight nose, large, violet eyes and clear-cut features, topped with masses of glossy brown hair, Constance was a natural replica. Her female relatives would be shocked as she, as a follower of the cult, jettisoned her bustle and whalebone in favour of Pre-Raphaelite contours, which were all the rage.

News arrived from home regularly, for the Victorians were great letter-writers, and the Lloyd cousins were no exception. Letters told of Oscar playing tennis at Bingham Rectory and making up to Frank Miles's pretty sisters. Brother Otho had decided to please his grandfather and chose a legal career instead of the classical one he had set his heart on. Uncle Charles Hemphill wrote from Dublin: ". . . Lady Wilde has sold the Merrion Square house—everything was mortgaged to the hilt, including the country residence of Moytura, and the row of houses at Bray—and is gone to launch herself on the great unheeding metropolis across the water. She wants Oscar to enter Parliament when he settles—he would get in on his mother's name alone, I should think. Willie is living with her in London, but Oscar has taken rooms off the Strand. . . ."

While abroad, the Pre-Raphaelites read of the upsurge of an Aesthetic Movement; some referred to it as the latest craze, but it was actually a natural consequence of Pre-Raphaelite thought. John Ruskin had announced years before that "Sensation, form, colour and feelings were meant to provide a refined pleasure for everyone."

The Aesthetic Movement was young. It was change. But it was not new. Plato had spoken of it, and the German philosophers regarded it as a science "which treats of the conditions of sensuous perception". The French had long since absorbed it into their culture, and now it had crossed the English Channel, where the distinction between sensuous perception and sensuous indulgence was dangerously slight.

By this time Constance Lloyd had stepped right out of the confines of her early upbringing; the maternal shackles had been shaken off, and the knowledge of a marriage settlement gave her a new confidence. The company in which she moved broadened her outlook considerably, for always gathered about the Ranee was an admiring crowd listening to her stories told with a shocking nonchalance.

"Of course, life in Borneo takes some getting used to," the Ranee told her audience, some of whom had never heard of this far-flung corner of empire. "Customs are different . . . values . . . habits. For instance, when I first went out it was terribly hot and humid, and people were hoping the rains would come and put an end to it." She puffed at her cigarette from a long holder and continued. "Well, we were sitting about on the verandah after dinner, hoping for the rain, when I heard a sound. The rain! I declared, leaping to my feet. The rain is coming, can you not hear it?" She paused, her mesmeric blue eyes sweeping the company. "The silence with which my words were greeted grew into a sea of amused glances and giggles . . . you can imagine how bewildered I was. I looked about, and do you know what it was?" They did not. "The sound which I thought was rain, was in fact, the Rajah relieving himself over the verandah rails!"

Aunt Emily and Mama would not have approved of such improper stories, or of the gossip and frankly discussed scandalous intrigues and extra-marital affairs which seemed to be a vital part of Continental society. Still less did her relatives approve of Constance's having refused 'good offers' of marriage. Who the suitors were is not known, and we might not have been aware of their existence except for a comment of one of the Irish aunts, who, on hearing of her nieces engagement to Oscar, declared that she had "turned down three good proposals to marry a man who looked like a third rate actor!" Vyvyan Holland suggests that one of these was Edward Heron Allen, her cousin Stanhope's friend, an eccentric young man by any standards. He was three years her junior and already possessed of wealth; he was also an astrologer and wrote a number of books on a variety of subjects which ranged from scientific tales to romances, from heraldry to asparagus culture! He never married but made violins, drew up horoscopes, became a lawyer and never practised, and read fat palms for fat fees in fashionable drawing-rooms.

The idyllic existence in Monaco was brought to an end by a letter from Aunt Mary Napier, who was determined to do the right thing by her niece. "You really must come home, now," she wrote. "Your Aunt Cornelia has very kindly arranged to bring you out . . . every girl needs a proper introduction into society." The aunt concerned was aunt in name only; she was a friend of the Ranee and wife of Admiral Sir Basil Cochrane. "So, Cornelia's launching you," joked the Ranee, "like one of Basil's battleships, eh, dressed overall!" Any account of the "launching"—if it was ever reported—cannot be traced.

Meanwhile, back in London, William S. Gilbert and Arthur Sullivan, whose partnership was already ten years old, had produced a new comic opera called *Patience*, which was a send-up of the new cult of Aestheticism. It must be said that the movement was, really, a serious, altruistic attempt to change the Victorian lifestyle. Naturally, the young people were all in favour of change—clothes, art, furniture, décor, they wanted something different. "Throw out your mahogany!" was one catch-phrase. Gloomy parlours with plush curtains and aspidistras were out. White paint, hand-printed materials and flowers were in. The strict, and often hypocritical, social conventions were questioned; and because the majority did not understand what it was all about, they either came down heavily against Aestheticism or lampooned it. Gilbert and Sullivan had originally decided to satirize curates in *Patience*, but it occurred to them that a satire on the cloth might not go down too well—so the curates were replaced by poets. Then the question arose—which poets? There were no lack of them. It was a toss-up as to whether they should have Swinburne, Walter Pater or even Whistler.

Constance returned to London to discover the town tapping its toe to the latest tunes from the operetta. It was considered to be "hilarious". Not only was the theme new but the Savoy Theatre had been especially built and was the first to be dazzlingly lit with the new electric lighting. In *Patience* the philistines gave their answer to Aestheticism and set the retort to rollicking music. The adjective which Ruskin had put about, "consummately", became the comic catch-word, and Pre-Raphaelite attitudes of adoration were stylized. The taste for early Italian art was made fun of: "How Botticellian, how Fra Angelican!" And it concludes with the poet relinquishing his "affectations" and becoming "a matter-of-fact young man".

Patience, then, was a send-up of the new cult, and it was Dante Gabriel Rossetti, and not the young Wilde, who was caricatured as the "fleshly poet" Bunthorne. The satirization took off in a big way, and as the cult grew in popularity, it became more and more the butt of popular, public humour. The pages of *Punch* were full of jokes about long-haired young men and how they were "finding it difficult to live up to blue china". Plays and poems were hurtling off the presses and onto the bandwagon. Barrel organs toured the streets grinding out the 'Magnet and the Churn', and tenors in drawing-rooms capered about with "a poppy or a lily in your medieval hand".

While Rossetti was nightly caricatured at the Savoy, Lillie Langtry was packing 'em in at the Lyceum—and Oscar Wilde, budding poet and aesthete, attended her every performance. He declared himself to be in love with her and proved his devotion by sleeping on her doorstep.

It was not only Lady Wilde who had come to launch herself "on the great unheeding metropolis" but her son as well. Not that the metropolis was unheeding. It was sitting up and taking notice of the large young man with amber-coloured hair, haughty, humorous eyes and the wonderful golden voice which he modulated with elaborate self-consciousness. He had even set up a studio with his friend the artist Frank Miles, whose father was the Rector of Bingham and whose sisters were exceedingly pretty—and everyone who was anyone attended their open afternoons, from the Prince of Wales, and Lillie

Langtry down to students and admirers like the Troubridge girls and Constance. What the latter thought of the rise to popularity of Grand-mama's one-time neighbour from Dublin is not recorded.

That it was Oscar and not Willie who was being patronized by theatrical and literary folk must have caused some surprise, for as a youth Oscar showed no inclination to commandeer the limelight, while Willie had been and still was a vivacious, witty and natural talker. In any case, Willie was out of the running altogether, for he wore a beard, and as every Aesthetic young woman would know, beards were out.

Laura Troubridge recorded in her diary that Oscar was "absolutely divine . . . more assured, amusing. . .". Aunt Emily would have used the word "affected", but then aunts did not understand Aesthetics. The studio was in a curious old house on the corner of Salisbury Street just off the Strand (it was demolished a couple of years later for re-development). Here Frank Miles, who was pioneering to bring back the herbaceous border and had a good reputation as a hybridizer of lilies, shared the long, low-ceilinged room with Oscar. Naturally, the air was heavy with scent of Frank's lilies; the atmosphere was informal, and the 'open teas' consisted of a variety of folk wandering about with cup and saucer in hand. Etchings and paintings vied with photographs of Mrs Langtry, and peacock-feather screens partitioned the studio. Back from her European travels, Constance could not fail to be impressed and, as an ardent Pre-Raphaelite, wasted no time at all in absorbing Aesthetic principles.

Living at Lancaster Gate meant she was free, duty visits apart, from the restrictions and temper of her mother, to enjoy not merely her Aesthetic leanings but the social life of the metropolis. Chaperoned by Aunt Mary Napier, there were soirées, dances, suppers, dinners, theatres, lectures or merely visiting with Grandpapa Lloyd. Occasionally she would discover that Oscar Wilde was attending the same functions as herself, as when the Thames overflowed its banks at Lambeth causing hundreds to be destitute and homeless, and Constance's set, plus a contingent of General Booth's Salvation Army, took part in the emergency relief work setting up soup kitchens—one of the young men engaged in carrying mattresses for the homeless was Oscar.

Another place at which Constance would not have expected to see him was a Theosophical Luncheon. Through both of them was a philosophical streak, almost bordering on superstition, due perhaps to the Irish in their natures. Attendance at the luncheon was merely the accepting of an invitation on his part, but Constance was immensely drawn to this new and interesting cult which was sweeping London. Or was it not so much the cult as its forceful and flamboyant exponent, Madam Blavatsky, who first aroused her interest? What a surprise, then, for Constance to see Mrs Isobel Cooper Oakley fetching Oscar over to talk, but it was not Oscar of the blazer and straw hat, nor was he wearing the impeccable afternoon clothes of the studio but silk knee-breeches, soft Byronical shirts, stockings and buckled shoes! "Ah, you didn't know I gave matinée performances, did you?" She obviously did not, so he followed it up with: "Not only do I give matinée performances, but while dining I am expected to deliver *bons mots* between mouthfuls!"

Constance found the Theosophical arguments for belief in re-incarnation simple and convincing and was certain that we can, in some way, affect our destiny. He, on the other hand, believed that "The gods mark out a path for us which we must follow to its conclusion." She might well have accused him of wallowing in the Calvinistic doctrine of predestination, had not Madam Blavatsky descended. Madam was a large woman with black eyes and an overpowering personality. On one occasion, when handing a butter-dish to her colleague-cum-arch enemy, Annie Besant, she thundered, "Here, grease your way to hell!" Her fingers seemed always to be engaged in rolling cigarettes, which she smoked one after the other, with scant regard for convention. "Have you not heard, Madam." teased Oscar, "that mediums are rolling cigarettes and talking black magic in the rooms of Cambridge dons until the hair of the undergraduates resembles that of a porcupine! Not to mention the three youths at Trinity who nearly poisoned themselves with hashish in an attempt to project their astral bodies—they were only saved by a rebellious tutor armed with a stomach pump." Madam's reply was apparently forestalled by the appearance of a young Indian gentlemen in a turban who called them to their appointed places at table.

There are several accounts written up as to when Oscar Wilde was formally introduced to the Lloyd family, and all are open to conjecture.

The event would not have taken place without a certain amount of natural trepidation on both his and Constance's part, for her relatives were bound to rake up old Dublin scandals of the past and look askance at the future. Her grandfather invited him to one of Aunt

Emily's 'At Homes', for he liked Oscar, and that was all that mattered. One can imagine the chesty old man chuckling, "See if he can charm your Aunt Emily, eh!"—but in that quarter he never succeeded.

About this time Oscar was working; that is, he had taken upon himself to civilize the provinces by giving a series of lectures on Aesthetics; for a fee of upward of 25 guineas per lecture, the pay was not all that bad. With subjects as unlikely to attract attention as 'The House Beautiful' and 'Aspects of Dress', he had the nerve to brave the boards of Birkenhead and Bradford, dressed in the height of Regency style and with his hair waved. There were cries of, "Get yer 'air cut!"

"Dandy Wilde!"

"Ya, Bunthorne!"

Not that any audience got the better of him, for after its first sense of bewilderment wore off, they laughed not at him but with him.

Descriptions of Wilde's extravagant appearance at this time are tempered with, "But his strong, humorous haughty eyes, his good brow and fine nose must not be forgotten from the general effect, and of course his wonderful golden voice. Exotic as he seemed, he was entirely different from the dilettante we had expected and the great surprise was his impudent humour and sound common sense. . . . There was an unquestionable fascination about the strange popinjay who even won our parents into the admission that he was no fool."

Wilde was saying all the things the young and intense had been feeling. The gospel he preached was an extension of what had been said at the Babbacombe Cliff gatherings. It was a precept of John Ruskin's to take culture to the masses, and, bearing as it did so authentic a stamp of approval, Constance Lloyd was a hundred per cent in agreement.

By 1881 she was, at Lady Wilde's request of course, a regular visitor at the Park Street salon. And what an asset she must have been; with her looks and style she was picture enough to delight and soften any formal gathering. Also, at this time, Oscar made himself available to be present at his mother's gatherings, partly to bask in praise of his recently published first book of poems. There is no doubt that salons, At Homes and afternoon teas provided a perfectly legitimate trysting-place for young people to talk and become further acquainted with each other—and that Constance and Oscar took full advantage of the facility. There would also be opportunity for him to enlarge upon his new enthusiasm for the theatre in the form of a play he had written called *Vera; or the Nihilists*—a drama, Terence de Vere White has said, of unique inadequacy. Constance, enmeshed in the spell of Oscar's mellow, persuasive voice, agreed to read it, for, after all, it was another link with him and provided fuel for further conversations.

Meanwhile, Aestheticism continued to flourish, and D'Oyly Carte—'Oily Cart' as he was nick-named—decided to take the Gilbert and Sullivan production of *Patience* to America. The citizens of that continent, however, had not heard of anything so refined as Aestheticism and could not understand its satirical content; consequently the box office was suffering. What they needed, D'Oyly Carte wrote, was "a real, live aesthete, preferably one who could lecture on the subject". Grandfather Lloyd's friend George Lewis, later Sir George, of the firm of solicitors Lewis & Lewis, suggested they send Oscar—or did old Mr Lloyd put the suggestion forward? Anyway, it was taken up at once—a chance not to be missed.

"I think you are very brave," declared one of the cousins to Oscar, no doubt echoing Constance's thoughts, "to go to a strange land, amongst strange people, to mount a stage, dressed . . . well, dressed as an aesthetic young man, and to lecture on the subject—I think you are very brave!"

"I am touched for your concern, Miss Napier," replied Oscar, "I must admit to a little apprehension, but after all," his smile widened to take in Aunt Emily, "they can't shoot me!"

"I should not be too sure about that, Mr Wilde!" was Aunt Emily's tart comment; and so the Apostle of Aestheticism sailed out on the *Arizona* on Christmas Eve.

5

An Engagement is Announced

That Oscar and Constance wrote to each other while he was in America is fairly certain, but none of the letters has come to light, and of course many were destroyed either by herself or by her family before the trial of 1895. With or without letters, the winter of 1882 must have passed with aggravating slowness for Constance. Rain, fog, snow and ice came and went. The social whirl must have been much less of a whirl without the anticipatory thrill or the likelihood of seeing Oscar at some of the season's functions.

The family at Lancaster Gate, and in Dublin, followed with interest the newspaper account of Oscar's tour, which had proved so successful that he was drawing a greater audience than the *Patience* he had been sent out to promote—and earning at some theatres £400 a lecture. His tour in America received very high Press ratings, and one in particular was from *Leslie's Illustrated News*, owned by Mrs Frank Leslie, who later married Oscar's elder brother, Willie. When Constance went down to stay that summer with Lady Mount Temple, her 'Mia Madre', or when she went to stay with Grandmama Atkinson, Oscar's success was sure to be a topic of conversation—what he was doing, saying, wearing. Nothing like him had hit the States in years, it seemed. Lady Wilde, always ambitious for her sons, was ecstatic.

Constance, we may be sure, did not allow her visits to the Park Street salon to lapse; how else could she keep in touch? There was always a warmth of affection between Constance and Lady Wilde, and one wonders whether, again, it was the theatrical flamboyance, the outré personality which grew on her. Lady Wilde had been a lonely woman since her husband's death, for despite their eccentricities there had been a warm bond of friendship between them, "a point", someone said, "in her idealism and his enthusiasm where their natures met". And now all her attention was on her sons. She went into raptures at Oscar's name being linked in American papers with the daughter of the authoress Mrs Julia Ward Howe and marvelled at the possible literary connection. But Oscar's name had been linked with girls before, either in love or in serious flirtations. H. Montgomery Hyde in his book *Oscar Wilde* quotes an indignant mother's letter:

> I was very much pained the last time I was at your house when I went into the drawing room and saw Fidelia sitting on your knee. Young as she is, she ought to have had—and I told her so—the instinctive delicacy that would have shrunk from it. But, oh, Oscar, the thing was neither right nor manly, nor gentlemanlike in you! You have disappointed me—nay so low and vulgar was it that I could not have believed anyone of refined mind capable of such a thing.

The outraged parent was further annoyed by Oscar leaving her to open the front door for herself, while he stayed behind in the hall to steal a surreptitious kiss from the apparently not unwilling Fidelia. This called forth another outburst: "Do you think for a moment that I was so supremely stupid as not to know that you always kissed Fidelia when you met her if you had an opportunity?"

Constance would have known of his serious affair some three years before with Florrie Balcombe, a Dublin girl, who turned him down to marry Bram Stoker instead. In the year his poems were published, he sent Florrie a copy; also, that same year, when Florrie got her first stage part, a walk-on in Irving's play *The Cup* at the Lyceum in January, Oscar sent to Ellen Terry, one of the leading ladies, two crowns of flowers. One was for herself and the other to give to Florrie without revealing from whence it had come. He wallowed in transports of tragic emotions about his past love, who, alas, did not take his devotion seriously enough. But it was a nice sentimental gesture not really meant for anonymity. It is safe to assume that Oscar, always extravagantly sentimental, hoped she would find out.

There were other, milder affairs, and with these in mind Constance would have suffered the thousand doubts and mild jealousies that being parted, and at such a distance, and with nothing even settled or declared, bring.

Meanwhile, Oscar, having finished a lecture on 'English Art', was surprised by the candid way in which the American young men in the hall gave him a nudge and said, "Now Oscar, after all the soulthrob, of course you feel like a bit of skirt" and took him off to a brothel.

What depressed Constance more than the Julia Ward Howe alliance was the rumour of his following the present tour with one to Australia—"Strike while the iron is hot," urged his agent. Lady Wilde's dearest wish regarding her sons was wealth for Willie—probably on account of his beginning to borrow money from her—for Oscar brilliance and fame, and for both of them wonderful wives. She was hopelessly worried about Willie's ever finding the right woman, for his engagement to Ethel Smythe had been brevity itself; he was drinking more than was good for him, and in danger of wrecking his career as a journalist. Marriage was certainly on her mind when she wrote to Oscar that their old neighbour from Merrion Square days, Charles Hemphill, paid her a visit: ". . . very pleasant. He praised Constance immensely. I had it in mind to say I would like her for a daughter-in-law, but I did not. It was Constance who told him where we lived. I thought his visit looked encouraging. He said you were quite a celebrity now."

It would appear that there was a bit of collusion between mother and son as to the possibility of bringing Constance into the family. The degree of intimacy is obvious in referring to the girl's Christian name and not the formality of 'Miss Lloyd'. The buttering-up of the young people, each to the other, bears strong hints of match-making, and Uncle Charles, being a favourite, would, no doubt, have been badgered and questioned by his niece as to how the visit went. It would have been a hard-hearted man who would not have dropped a hint which sent her into a happily nervous state—for the old year was nearly at an end, and the new one would bring Oscar Wilde back from his successful American tour.

He returned, as Uncle Charles had said, a celebrity. He was a lot better off financially, and the success sat as easily on his broad shoulders as the great fur coat he brought back from the States. At this time he wore his hair long—collar length. It was thick and parted in the middle—High Church style. Fame added assurance to his fascin-ating personality, and he had discovered that the scent of violets was to be his own personal perfume. How could Constance fail to fall in love with him? Surely her taste for the outré would be satisfied with the Apostle of Aestheticism? As for him, always a man to appreciate female beauty, her large violet-coloured eyes and Pre-Raphaelite looks, the distinctive low tone of her voice, masses of brown hair and slender Grecian figure, seemed worth coming home to.

Cosy talks at Lancaster Gate or walks in the park were not of too long a duration, for almost at once his agent fixed another series of lectures. He had to "ride the wave of popularity" which his American promotion of *Patience* had brought. "Strike while the iron is hot," said the agent. Constance must have thanked God that the iron was to be struck not in Australia but in the provinces. "Charity begins at home," he had quipped. What form their courtship took is not known, but in the following year their relationship was furthered. His absences would bring letters; his presence would bring "hilarity", as the term went. The Victorians had ways of communicating, despite chaperones, and Oscar was the kind who would steal a kiss at the least opportunity, while Constance, as her later letters show, needed no encouraging to comply.

In August Oscar embarked at Liverpool for America again, this time for the opening of his play *Vera*, or, to give it its full title, *Vera, or the Nihilists*. The play was an instant flop. It ran for only a week and received scathing reviews. Oscar returned hot-foot.

Romance was in the air that year. Otho announced his engagement to a young and lively lady named Nellie Hutchinson, whom none of the family, even Constance, appeared to have met. It seemed the prerogative of sons to be capable of springing sudden engagements to unknown people on their unprepared and unsuspecting families, and Otho was no exception. He who had never appealed to his sister for anything before was now dependent on her not only to break the ice formed by his sudden engagement but to make sure a definite thaw had set in by the time he brought Nellie to meet the family. Perhaps Otho suspected that his sister and Oscar Wilde were just a little more than good friends and that in the future she might need him to do some thawing-out on her behalf! He had another pressing reason for wanting his sister to sweeten things on the home front. He had incurred his grandfather's displeasure by deciding, after all, not to follow the family profession in law but to revert to his original inclination for the life of a classical scholar.

If Constance envied her brother's engagement, her turn was soon to come. Was it purely coincidence that Oscar happened to be lecturing in Dublin at the time she was visiting her grandmother? If the event had not been pre-arranged between the two, it was either good management on her part or a stroke of amazing luck.

The visit took place in November 1883, and no sooner had Constance set foot in Ely Place than her cousins gathered like vultures to tease her unmercifully about Oscar. There was no doubt at all that news concerning the state of her friendship with him had regularly crossed the Irish Sea in the form of letters from Eliza. Constance, however, was really in no mood to be teased, for Oscar had only three days in town. Three days, and he, being a Dubliner born and bred, was in great demand. She read in the newspapers of his dining with the Fellows of Trinity, addressing the Royal Academy, giving a poetry recital and being in public debate with the Reverend John Pentland Mahaffy, his old tutor, with whom he had been touring Greece while she, with Lady Mount Temple, had been touring Italy. Oscar, equally desperate, had booked a box to see the comic opera *The Merry Duchess* at the Gaiety Theatre and invited Constance and the cousins to join him, but again his engagements came between them, and he was unable to attend.

The cousins thought it no end of a lark and followed the progress of his doings with more than a passing interest. They urged Constance to invite him to Ely Place so they could all take a closer look at him and satisfy their curiosity. After all, a local boy who made such an impression in London was bound to be of interest. Consequently, Stanhope, son of Charles Hemphill, left a note at the Sherborne Hotel where Oscar was staying, inviting him to call at Ely Place. Victorian afternoon teas were rather stiff affairs, and under the circumstances Oscar must have felt the strain of the formality—not to mention the curious and appraising eyes of his contemporaries and the shrewd, assessing glance of Mrs Atkinson and the aunts. As for Constance, she too was in a highly nervous state, hoping he would say just the right things and not put on too much of a pose. She need not have worried, for, never a one to overplay his part, and looking handsome in Norfolk jacket and tweed trousers, he charmed them all so much that the cousins invested two shillings each at the theatre to attend both his lectures. The first, on 22nd November, was entitled 'The House Beautiful' and contained revolutionary schemes of an aesthetic nature for house décor.

The second, 'Personal Impressions of America', was, of course, about his tour. Being in love with the lecturer had not blinded Constance's judgement, for she did not reckon the 'Personal Impressions of America' to be as good as the former.

During the busy week-end, and sandwiched between his social engagements, Oscar conspired to get his beloved on her own and propose marriage. She happily accepted, and they were so deliriously happy that they announced their engagement straight away. It has been said that Oscar proposed while Constance was playing the piano in the drawing-room at Ely Place, but one cannot imagine him being so conventional, especially with all those giggling cousins about. The engagement ring which he had had made several weeks before in London was an intricate affair which he had designed himself.

Brimming over with happiness, Constance's first letter was not to her favourite aunt, Mary Napier, nor to 'Mia Madre' at Babbacombe, nor yet to Grandpapa Lloyd, but to her brother Otho. It was not so much a rush of sisterly affection which prompted the letter as a strategic move on her part. Although Grandmama Atkinson and most of the Irish family approved of Oscar, she knew that the London family in general, and Aunt Emily in particular, would need softening up a little. Who better to do this than Otho, who was already in London and available to do the decent thing—she had done as much for him. Of one thing she was certain. Her mind was made up about Oscar, and whatever objections the family had would be totally disregarded. Despite her determination, when Oscar left Dublin on Monday morning, he took some of her courage with him. He was to continue his civilizing of the provinces, so there was no chance of his putting in an appearance at Lancaster Gate until the week-end.

The Irish Sea presented a terrible barrier between Constance and her newly announced love. Her decision to follow almost at once to London was assisted by the Irish relatives wanting to know how and why, and where they would live, and what prospects were there for a young man in London. It is understandable that someone should remind her of, or warn her about, the Wildes' family failings; about Sir William's infidelities, as though marital infidelity was a hereditary disease; and how Willie was drinking and womanizing to ruin himself. But Constance well knew her own mind; besides, her own family had its share of scandals: her father had his failings, but she loved him none the less, and Grandpapa's aberration of yesteryears did not make him less lovable. Constance knew what kind of love she wanted, or else why wait until she was twenty-six? Many married younger in those days. Having seen the result of her parents' unhappiness, and indeed spoiled for 'ordinary' marriage by her association with the Pre-Raphaelites, Constance stood her ground. Quiet she may have looked, as did indeed most early photographs of Victorian girls, but she knew what she wanted, and that was Oscar.

The weekend at Lancaster Gate appeared to have been a tremendous success, and Grandpapa Lloyd, who had been confined to his bed, declared that the engagement had got him on his feet again. Otho and Nellie, Constance's allies, were present to counteract the disapproval of Aunt Emily, and there would be Eliza and Aunt Mary and Auntie Carrie and numerous other London cousins. It did not matter if her mother did not exactly dance for joy or if Mr King remained silent, for Oscar was there beside her—and people in love can face anything together.

The Christmas season with its attendant fun and festivities heightened their new-found happiness. Oscar described her to his friends in rapturous phrases; and, of course, Lady Wilde was delighted with the engagement. There was no doubt that the engaged couple were very much in love and exceedingly happy in each other's company. She showed him off to all her friends and was the envy of every aesthetic young miss. He mooned about after her, waiting for her while she went into shops, and as a lover he had, and displayed, all those irresistible gestures that a girl deeply in love looks for.

Constance went overboard with love, for until going to Babbacombe Cliff she had not been encouraged to be extravagant in her emotions. She had never been idolized and adored in the extreme way the Wildes had loved their daughter Isola, and although her grandparents were kind and loved her, it was not at all the same thing. One could safely say that, if Constance had not lived with Lady Mount Temple, the Ranee and the effervescent Alice of Monaco and their kind, she would have grown to be as emotionally inarticulate as her parents had been, and quite unable to cope with or respond to Oscar's extravagant adoration. As it was, she did not do too badly. She confessed to being mad with love for him; wanting to bind him to her with chains of love; wanting to touch and hold him and run her fingers through his amber hair. He was accused of taking her sleep away with him, for she, like many other victims of Cupid, could not sleep for thinking about her Oscar. Oscar, the dreamy-eyed brother of Isola; the student eager and serious on Trinity Green; boyish in blazer and flannels; the Apostle of Aestheticism, and now the man she was going to marry.

This was the age of telegrams, the swift postal amenity which often ran to not a few terse words but pages. While he was away lecturing, they exchanged telegrams twice a day, and at every available opportunity he would hurry back to London just to be with her, even if only for a couple of hours. Propriety forbade Oscar to see Constance in his own rooms, but at Lancaster Gate there was, with the help of Henry, the butler, a little time to be alone together. Happy hours were spent in wrangling over questions of morality and art, after which, despite Oscar's persuasive tongue, she still maintained that it was possible for the two to go hand in hand.

Between Oscar and Constance there was a certain rapport; as time went on it became less certain, but it was always there. The reason, surely, being their past. He would not have been happy to struggle for his share of the limelight with a partner as brilliant as himself. A man of his temperament needed an oasis where he could relax and be himself—even geniuses cannot be on the stage all the time! While she needed someone in whom she could live out the fantasies, the aesthetic concepts, which, due to her conventional upbringing, had been denied her. Only in her visits to Babbacombe Cliff and to the Ranee did she really come alive, and now with Oscar a fantastic dream of Pre-Raphaelite quality lay ahead. This was the man for whom she had waited, for whom she had turned down "good offers". As yet, he had no profession, no job, apart from seasonal lecture tours, no expectations, and his published poems brought him very little money. None of that mattered. She had faith in him, encouraged and wished and believed that he would become famous.

They had many things in common: their families, their backgrounds; they knew of each other's scandals and did not mind. They shared a love of Keats's poetry, art, artists, theatre, music, and in the early undergraduate days he would have gone on about his Greek travels and raved about Cardinal Newman and the Roman Catholic Church, while she, in turn, would have told of her Italian travels—he was in Florence about the same time, but they had never met. There would be fascinating tales of John Ruskin, whom she had met and he never did, and anecdotes of the Ranee and her parrots, of Alice, of her beloved 'Mia Madre'—all of whom he had yet to meet. (Her friends were to come in very handy every now and again.) Perhaps her description of Babbacombe Cliff gave them the idea of decorating their house in Tite Street in a manner as unique, although not as grand.

Philippe Jullian, in his book *Oscar Wilde*, suggests that Oscar was trying to mould his betrothed into some Pre-Raphaelite ideal, as William Morris and John Ruskin had done—a kind of marriage *à la* Pygmalion, and that he wanted to make her into the most accomplished woman of her time. As previously stated, a rival as close as a wife would never have suited him. Besides, taking into consideration her mature age of twenty-six—and not sixteen as Ruskin's ideal had been—the fact of her already having been moulded by the Mount Temple circle, that she was cultured, beautiful and well read, that she had her quiet independence, her own views on art and morality, which opposed some of his—and stubbornness in view of all this, and with the Holland temper thrown in, Oscar would have been mad even to think of it. Constance had inherited that grave look of quiet reserve from her father, but, like him, what went on behind it was something quite different.

Jimmy Whistler, the artist, was in the habit of giving Sunday morning breakfast parties, and on 26th December, the *World* reported, "Mr. Whistler's last Sunday breakfast of the year was given in honour of two happy couples, Lord Garmoyle and his fairy queen, and Oscar and the lady whom he has chosen to be the Chatelaine of the House Beautiful"—the latter being the name of one of Oscar's lectures on house décor.

Not withstanding the honour, Constance did not care particularly for James McNeil Whistler and his waspish wit. He was small and wiry, and his hair was black and oily—with the exception, that is, of a carefully trained and obedient snow-white lock to which he owed a certain amount of fame. Possessing an artistic opinion of her own, Constance did not agree with her fiancé that Whistler was the greatest painter. As it happened, neither of the 'happy couples' lived happily ever after. The Lord Garmoyle mentioned was a mere callow youth of twenty-two and his fiancée possibly younger. He broke off his engagement to his fairy queen, an actress, who promptly sued him for breach of promise. She was awarded a record sum of £10,000. His lordship then married a clergyman's daughter and in 1890, while Oscar was on the brink of fame, died of pneumonia at the age of twenty-eight.

It was on crowded formal occasions such as the Sunday breakfast that she caught her first glimpse of what her future life could be: hostess to poets and painters, writers and other interesting people who gathered about Oscar. Not that she aspired to the heights of famous society hostesses—what would be the use when her husband was the epitome of wit?

All too soon the Christmas season had ended, the New Year was upon them, and Oscar had to continue his lecture tour. Constance, booted, muffed and fur-trimmed against the cold, bade her love farewell at the railway station. The past two weeks of being together, house-hunting, visiting and enjoying the social whirl had been so hectic and hilarious that the following days must have been as bleak as the January weather. The continuous arrival of flowers, telegrams and letters only served to heighten his absence. She kept the flowers alive far beyond their usual span, tending them as Keats's Isabella had tended her pot of basil.

In the New Year Grandpapa Lloyd sent for his solicitor, Sidney Hargrove, of Victoria Street, Westminster, to add a codicil to his Will drawn up in 1880, in the form of a marriage settlement.

By March Oscar and Constance had decided to take the house which is now 34 Tite Street but which was then 16.

In April Constance's grandfather sent for Sidney Hargrove again, this time to add a second codicil, adding £500 each to the sum already assigned for Horace's children. The wedding date had been fixed, and the invitations to an Aesthetic wedding were sent out.

6

An Aesthetic Wedding

While Constance and her cousins were taken up with frenzied re-checking of the guest list, with hurried visits to milliners, dress-makers, haberdashers and mantle makers, with last-minute consulta-tions with the bridesmaids, and a frantic re-ordering of the tiered wedding cake (due to an oversight at the cake shop, which in turn was due to the baker having ran off with the proprietor's daughter), Oscar was equally embroiled and exasperated in supervising the progress of the re-designing of the House Beautiful. Lack of progress was a more appropriate assessment, for he tried hurrying E. W. Godwin, the architect, who was not given to hurrying, and chivvying the work-men, who were not inclined to work. Oscar had, by now, finished his lecturing, and he and Constance were inseparable for the few weeks before the wedding. He would even have gone to see the final fitting of her gown, but Lady Wilde expressly forbade any such thing on the grounds of it being unlucky.

Oscar Wilde and Constance Lloyd were married by special licence at St James's Church, Sussex Gardens, on 29th May 1884 at 2.30 p.m. There was only one regret: old Horatio Lloyd was ill again and could not attend the marriage of his favourite granddaughter. The day was fine and warm, but there was a slight chill to the wind, which was unusual for early summer. It was the Whit weekend, and everyone seemed in a high holiday mood.

Whistler sent a telegram: "Fear I may not reach you in time for ceremony—don't wait." And Oscar made jokes about the crowded church being "a full house". Accounts of the wedding vary, not only between biographers but in newspaper reports. Some say Lady Wilde was in grey, others in red. One account refers uncharitably to Constance's hair as "frizzled"; another states that Oscar chose her wedding gown. The only part he had in the choice of the gown was the suggestion of a high Medici collar, which she accepted, and no doubt thereby began the spate of rumours that he designed everything.

The Aesthetic wedding has been referred to as "more like a theatrical spectacle", but then aren't they all? It was not always the custom for brides to wear white, and Constance wore a gown of pale yellow. The Medici collar, high at the back of her neck, tapered to a low-cut bodice and gave a touch of regality to the outfit. The folds of the skirt fell simply in true Pre-Raphaelite style to be gathered about her waist in a silver girdle, the gift of the bridegroom. Four of her cousins were bridesmaids, and leading the bridal procession were two little girls in wide Gainsborough hats. Silk gooseberry-gowns, with large sashes about their tiny waists, fell into straight folds to the ankles, displaying small, bronzed, high-heeled shoes. Long yellow gloves and bouquets of lilies made them look as if they had just stepped out of a Joshua Reynolds canvas in order to be there.

By 3 p.m. the Reverend Abbott had pronounced Oscar and Constance man and wife. "For better or worse", she was now Mrs Oscar Wilde, and her life from that moment was to be inextricably bound up with his.

Crowds had gathered outside the church. They had come to see an Aesthetic wedding, and they were not disappointed. Sixty-year-old 'Speranza', dressed in high theatrical style, was the epitome of regality. She enjoyed the day as if it were her own: "At least, I have a wonderful wife for one of my sons." Lady Mount Temple, Constance's beloved 'Mia Madre', had returned from Switzerland especially for the occasion, and the bride must have felt surrounded by love. Amid a welter of congratulations they rode in an open carriage to Lancaster Gate, where butler Henry Riches had prepared a light reception. Later the bridal couple were seen off by their friends at Charing Cross, where the boat-train bore them away on what was grandly called their 'wedding tour'.

The first part of the 'tour' was spent in Paris and the second at Dieppe. The fine weather did not last; it was nearing the end of the Paris season, and the Grand Prix that year was spoiled by rain, the cold and wind converting the fêtes into exhibitions of overcoats and umbrellas.

The honeymoon was spent at the Hotel Wagram, a modest establishment on the rue de Rivoli. Their apartment of three rooms overlooked the gardens of the Tuileries, which at night-time looked particularly enchanting. The lamps on the gates seemed to bloom and expand into golden chrysanthemum-like flowers, the trees wore garlands of tiny coloured lanterns—beneath the flickering lights lovers strolled hand in hand. To rise late, to dress hurriedly and engage in silly chit-chat and quick kisses while swallowing coffee, and then to emerge into the real world, elegant, serious and sober, is the prerogative of all lovers, and the Wildes were no exception.

Constance, looking radiant and wearing an exquisite creation which set every head turning, was enjoying herself immensely. Accompanied by the impeccably dressed Oscar, swinging a silver-topped cane, she presented herself to the public at large. The Eiffel Tower, the Bois de Boulogne, the Sacré Cœur: Constance was familiar with them all, but, heightened by the consciousness of love, they achieved another dimension of splendour. With Oscar's arm tucked lightly beneath her elbow, they strolled about the exhibition of the fantastically rich French painter Meissonier. Then in the evening to the opera; and another evening to the theatre where the new version of *Macbeth* had suffered terribly in translation and was redeemed only by the artistic genius of the great Sarah Bernhardt.

At the salon of Henrietta Ruebell, a celebrated Paris hostess and patron of the arts, Constance was introduced to a young man whom Oscar had previously met while lecturing in Chicago, a sculptor called John Donaghue. She was attracted to him at once, admired his Roman nose and Irish eyes and talked about Dublin while Oscar threw in jokes about America. It was not only his looks she admired—his work appealed to her as well. He seemed to have a good line in bronze bas-relief pieces, and she was greatly taken with one of a naked young boy playing a harp. Donaghue was also to execute an over-mantel for the House Beautiful.

To obtain a flavour of the eccentric celebrities about at the time, one has only to read William Rothenstein's description of Henrietta Ruebell: "A striking figure, with her bright red hair crowning an expressive but unbeautiful face, her fingers and person loaded with turquoise stones. In face and figure she reminded me of Queen Elizabeth—if one can imagine an Elizabeth with an American accent and a high, shrill voice like a parrot's.''

Some of Wilde's biographers have taken the fact of Constance enjoying her freedom as a married woman to mean that she was already tired of her husband! This was not so. She was pleased to be enjoying the freedom from the restrictive practices of being an unmarried Victorian female. Marriage was a passport into a new status. A whole code of do's and don'ts no longer applied. One could walk and travel alone; gone was the need for chaperones. Gone, for Constance, was the tedious advice given by well-meaning aunts. She was now, by right, her own mistress, not answerable to anyone, and she obviously felt free to express her interest in the good-looking men who came her way—which from the lips of a maiden lady would be considered quite improper.

Hilarity seems to have been the keynote of this whirlwind beginning, for when Constance reached out for the coffee-pot one morning, a young man had called to breakfast. He was another of Oscar's friends, by the name of Robert Sherard. He was a hard-up journalist and the great-grandson of the poet Wordsworth. Later he was Wilde's first biographer, but on this occasion he was the embarrassed confidant of an enthusiastic account of how Oscar and Constance had spent their first night together.

Sherard was also to relate an incident when the three of them, having dined out, were going for a drive in an open cab. They had reached the place de la Concorde when Robert insisted he wanted to throw his walking-stick away. When asked why he wanted to do such a thing, he replied, "It's a swordstick and for the last few moments I've had a wild desire to pull it out and plunge it through you. I think it is because you are so happy." Wilde thought the throwing out of the stick would create a fuss—he was not a one for scenes—but Constance laughed and took it out of Robert's hand. "I shall keep this," she said, and the little cane was, for a long time, one of her curiosities.

Oscar was not without previous sexual experience, as we know from his sampling the brothels of Paris and America, not to mention his first encounter as an undergraduate at Oxford with the campus prostitute 'Old Jess', from whom he contracted syphilis. After undergoing treatment, he was pronounced cured. Constance, being twenty-six when she married, would be aware that men came to the marriage bed with some degree of experience. Victorian girls tended either to know 'nothing', as Lady Bracknell put it, or 'everything', and considering her travels on the uninhibited Continent, with outspoken people, what with gossip and scandals, Constance would not be like the young Margaret de Windt who, on marrying Charles Brooke, went to bed wondering what on earth was going to happen!

Everyone seems agreed that the young Wildes were very much in love and that Constance came to the marriage with as much passion as he. Her letters, reveal a depth of emotion uninhibited by primness, modesty or other ladylike sentiments. No wonder Oscar was boasting about the wedding night! Robert Sherard further relates how, that morning, while passing through the Marché St-Honoré, Oscar stopped to buy up all the loveliest blooms off a flower stall and sent them, with a word of love on his card, to the bride he had left but a very short while ago. Such extravagance was not unusual. An aunt gave them a wedding present of £50, and with it they bought, of all things, "one exquisite silver spoon". An apostle spoon at that!

The final part of their wedding tour was spent at Dieppe, that fascinating watering-place so much loved and inhabited by artists. Alice, the scintillating young widow of the Duc de Richelieu, who had taught Constance to improve her Liszt, was there with her friend Lady Brooke, the Ranee of Sarawak. Constance was proud of her friendship with these two gifted and extraordinary women and was pleased to see how impressed Oscar was with their company.

Among the gathering at Dieppe were Princess Pignatelli and her daughter Olga Alberta, whose father was reputed to be the Prince of Wales. But for Constance the fact of Princess Pignatelli's having known Horace Lloyd, her own father, eclipsed by far any other interest. So, while Constance was charmed by the princess's recollections of her father, Oscar charmed Alice, whose interest in the theatre matched his own.

The newly wedded pair left Dieppe in the highest of spirits. The easy-going, indolent, carefree atmosphere had seeped into their souls, insulating them for a few more hours from the everyday concerns of life. That they had nowhere to live, the fact of separation when Oscar began a new course of lectures, the absence of money and no immediate prospects of any, was not of current concern—until they arrived at Charing Cross station.

The house in Tite Street being nowhere near ready and because they had nowhere else to live, Oscar had telegraphed his brother

Willie to book a room for them at a hotel. But when Willie met them at
the station, they came down to the realities of life rather quickly, with
Oscar exclaiming irritably, "You've booked us in at the Brunswick!
My God, Willie, they want two guineas a day. Didn't you try any-
where else?" Apparently Willie had, but the tourist season was at its
height and nothing else was available. Oscar was not amused and let
his brother know it. They quarrelled easily, and Constance was in no
mood to allow that. She liked the big, bearded man who was her
brother-in-law, and poured oil over what easily might have become
troubled waters by suggesting they stay with her people at Lancaster
Gate. Oscar was still not amused, probably on account of Aunt Emily,
but as she pointed out, it was either that or two guineas a day at the
Brunswick! There is no doubt that Constance had a sense of
humour—there are many fascinating glimpses of it in what few letters
there are left. Humour is an individual thing, and without some form
of it she would not have lasted long with the sophisticated wit of the
Ranee and her circle. It has been levelled against Constance, by some
of her husband's admirers, that she did not laugh at his jokes; she had
probably heard them so often that they no longer amused her. Her
little joke mollified Willie, who hired a cab for them and followed it up
with an invitation to the theatre and then to dine with his latest
conquest.

It is not difficult to imagine the newly-weds, homeless and wanting
to cadge a few nights' lodging on the cheap. It was mid-afternoon. The
day was hot. Lancaster Gate seemed deserted; not even a leaf stirred.
Standing on the top step of the white-stuccoed house with its pillars
and balconies, it must have had more of an atmosphere of a hotel than
a home. A few moments later, when the butler opened the door and
they were standing in the cool, commodious hall, he informed them in
suitably muted tones that her grandfather was very ill and that his
doctor did not hold out much hope of a recovery. It was indeed reality.
To make matters worse, Constance's best ally of the London aunts,
the Honourable Mrs Napier, was out of town. Aunt Emily was resting
and pointedly remained undisturbed in her room. But Auntie Carrie,
who liked Constance well enough, although Otho was her favourite,
welcomed them to stay for tea. There was news to exchange and catch
up on and, there seems to have been a jinx on the Lloyd wedding
cakes. The baker 'running off' with the proprietor's daughter had
almost jeopardized Constance's cake, but Otho's never arrived at all!
Her brother had married Nellie Hutchinson on 10th June, just two

weeks after the Wilde wedding. What reason there was for the brother and sister not to arrange their respective dates so they could attend each other's wedding is not known; however, they had taken lodgings at not too great a distance, so there would be ample opportunity for Oscar to meet Nellie. There were also wedding presents arranged in Aunt Emily's neatest manner—a manner which forbade the invasion of eager hands. Nevertheless, invasion took place, reducing the neat spectacle to a heap. Eventually, after hints—jocular, of course, about the high price of accommodation: "the extortionate price of a bench in Hyde Park—as for the embankment!"—they were allowed to stay for a few days.

Although her grandfather was well into his eighties, the fact of his 'sinking' clouded Constance's evening at the Avenue Theatre with the charming Willie and the engaging little Madame Gabrielle. It is said he wore a bracelet she had given him, remarking that it was a "gift of the Gab"!

After a few uncomfortable days at Lancaster Gate, Oscar arranged for them to move into his old bachelor rooms at 9 Charles Street, Grosvenor Square. The oak-panelled apartments were really for 'young gentlemen', but the kindly ex-butler, Mr Davis, and his wife made an exception for the "nice Mr Wilde".

Constance, while dwelling on the lack of money in their lives, made some comments which have left her open to misjudgement by critics, some who poke fun at her idea of "becoming an actress, reporter, or novelist in case of need". To begin with, she has been misquoted, for, 'becoming an actress' is entirely different from what was meant by 'going on the stage'. Constance was not the only one to make such a statement; the artist, Louise Jopling also entertained the idea, and both did indeed tread the boards. There was at the time a spate of theatrical productions of the Attic variety performed either in or out of country houses. Lady Archie Campbell, along with the architect Edward Godwin, was responsible for the phenomenon. Her ladyship was a pioneer of open-air drama, for which she needed crowd scenes of graceful and beautiful women to take the part of sylphs, nymphs and handmaidens. This extract from a report gives a good impression of what was meant by 'going on the stage'. The play was *Helena in Troas*.

"With the death of Paris . . . the play was not yet over, for when, like figures on a marble frieze, the band of white-robed maidens wound past the altar, and one by one in slow procession climbed the steps and passed away, the audience were absolutely stilled in their excitement." Both Constance and Louise Jopling appeared in this kind of production.

As for becoming a reporter, she would have been a good one, for the coverage she did for the magazines *To-day*, *World* and *Ladies' Pictorial* makes interesting reading. She had a light, humorous style, an asset in all the ponderous prose of the day. Apart from the articles, she wrote a story-book for small children and for many years edited the *Rational Dress* magazine. (Healthful clothes were as much the rage then as health foods are now.) Later she was to make a selection of her husband's work and publish it under the title of *Oscariana*.

The following week, on 18th July, John Horatio Lloyd QC died at the age of eighty-four. Constance felt the loss not only of a beloved grandparent but of an ally. He had taken her to live with him; he had sheltered her from the heaviness of the Dublin family; and his financial assistance had rescued her and Otho from being dependent upon the charity of aunts and uncles. John Horatio Lloyd, who, up to the end, had so much zest for life, was no more.

On the 23rd, the blinds were drawn at Lancaster Gate as the black-plumed horses bore his body in the hot sun to Hendon Cemetery, where he was buried with all the attendant pomp and ceremony befitting the originator of Lloyd's Bonds. At Lancaster Gate, the funeral guests, under the stimulus of butler Henry's refreshing wines and cold collation, would, no doubt, stand about in clusters, some to consider his monetary value, some to commiserate and others to console.

The gross value of his personal estate was £92,392 4s 1d, the executors being Aunt Emily and his nephew Horatio Lloyd, Recorder of Chester. The estate was divided into four parts, one to each of his three daughters, and the fourth share to be put in trust and divided between Otho and Constance, "independently of any husband". This latter clause applied to the aunt's share also. There were also the two codicils previously mentioned, one of which was the marriage settlement.

Otho was given the choice of any of his grandfather's prize and classical books. Emily, apart from the house, was bequeathed silver goblets which had belonged to his father, the Prothonotary who put down the Blanketeers, and his father-in-law, Major Holland Watson; also an oil painting of himself presented by Sir George Elliot, Baronet, and all other silver, liqueurs, wines and household effects. Auntie Carrie was to have the marble bust of himself and whatever Emily did not want, and Aunt Mary Napier was to retain the house and furniture her father had bought for her, probably when she was widowed eight years before. There was future income from stocks and shares to be apportioned and the proceeds from an auction of unwanted goods and chattels. Horace's wife, Adele, was not mentioned. The outcome was that Constance could expect £800 a year from the estate, for life, which was not a fortune but came in very handy all the same and served, as her grandfather had intended, to give her a measure of independence. If the old man had not put the money in trust and added the clause "independent of any husband", she would have been in dire straits later on.

Early in July, before the death of Mr Lloyd, the newly-weds went to tea with Laura Troubridge, a young lady who, although neither knew it at the time, was to become a feature of Constance's life. She wrote in her diary: "July 1884, Mr and Mrs Oscar Wilde to tea. She dressed for the most part in limp white muslin with NO bustle, saffron coloured silk swathed about her shoulders, a huge cartwheel hat, white and bright yellow stockings and shoes—she looked too hopeless and we thought her shy and dull. He was amusing of course." Laura had met Oscar some five years before, at a tea given by her cousin Charles Orde; she had thought him quite delightful then, but now her adjective had come down the scale to describe him merely as 'amusing'. Her reference to Constance being dull is a favourite description of hers, for in her diary two years later she noted that the young man soon to become her fiancé, Adrian Hope, had, in the company of the same cousin, Charles, lunched with Oscar and a brother and sister called Sickert, who were "both hideous and very dull". In actuality Walter and Helena Sickert were far from this description. They were life-long friends of Oscar's—Helena had shared skating lessons with him in Dublin. She had since taken a degree at Girton and, apart from writing and lecturing, was an untiring advocate of Women's Rights. Lively, witty, intelligent, it was all lost on Laura and Adrian. Helena married F. T. Swanwick in 1888, the same year that Laura married Adrian. As for Walter Sickert, he was an artist, a disciple of Whistler, and painted lusty scenes of the working classes enjoying themselves in gilded music halls.

Constance's gown came in for criticism because it was an aesthetic creation. Besides, to appear without a bustle was considered indelicate; moreover limp muslin clung to the contours, and bright colours were out. As for appearing "shy", it must be remembered that

Constance Wilde inherited a look of quiet reserve from her father, and like him, once having the measure of the company, she became a charming young woman with a subtle sense of humour. It is interesting to note that, when the Wildes were famous, Laura was not averse to drawing portraits of their children or going to see Oscar's plays with her "shy and dull" relative by marriage.

Laura and her young man, Adrian, although a delightful pair, were very 'establishment', very respectable and conventional. Anything they did not understand was subject to ridicule. From clothes to house to attitude, anything which deviated from the norm was suspect. The limp white muslin, apart from enhancing Constance's figure, was part of the healthy clothes regime to which both the Wildes subscribed and would have been much cooler and healthier in the heat of July than the corded silk gowns and leg-of-mutton sleeves of the day.

By the autumn Oscar had resumed his lecture tours; they were short of money with which to feed the house in Tite Street. Its appetite was enormous, due to the epicurean diet, and like any young marrieds they longed to see it grow into the house of their dreams. Oscar had to direct the operations by post; everything had to be just so, for he who lectured on the 'House Beautiful' could scarcely live in less.

The *Bristol Times and Mirror* described him on 16th October as "a well built good looking gentleman, dressed in perfectly fitting black frock coat and light trousers, with a naturally dignified yet withall easy and graceful manner, and who delivers his lecture in a resonant and musical voice, and in a highly interesting style".

By travelling overnight Oscar contrived to be back at their rooms in Charles Street for a long weekend. There were urgent matters to be settled, such as the choice of colour schemes; and the only person who could help resolve this burning question was the elusive but extremely gifted Edward Godwin. Contrary to what Oscar thought, there were other things in Godwin's life beside the refurbishing of 16 Tite Street. While the young Wildes fretted and fumed in their eagerness to take up residence, Godwin was either taking a cure at a popular hydropathic establishment, or indulging his artistic expertise by producing one of Lady Archie Campbell's pastoral plays. It was all very convenient, for the gardens of the said establishment at Coombe were ideal for the forest scenes from *As You Like It*, which were perfomed in the July of 1884 and in May 1885. These productions were followed by the *Faithful Shepherdess* and *Fair Rosamund*.

As it happened, there was not only the colour scheme to be settled but the £200.17s.0d. contractor's bill—all of it. Godwin had under-estimated the initial cost, and the contractors, by the name of Green, stopped work and downed tools until their bill was settled. It was already November, and while the matter was being subject to the tardy processes of law, they employed another man called Sharpe. Meanwhile, the new furniture began to arrive at Tite Street—but the wily Green, the first contractor, seized it and other pieces and announced his intention of hanging on to them until his bill was paid in full. Then the new contractor sent in his account, which drove Oscar to write in desperation to Edward Godwin.

The actual legal proceedings over the contractor's bill dragged on until the following May, when a settlement was agreed; with costs and all, the Wildes were £250 out of pocket. Constance wrote too, appeal-ing to their dapper little friend to look out for an artistic bath for her room; clearly, nothing of a commonplace nature was to be installed.

The house which was to be Constance's home for the next ten years was at last ready. Like all newly-weds they were anxious to move in to their very own place, and Constance more so, for by now she was four months pregnant. 16 Tite Street received much publicity at the time, especially in magazines, on account of its being an example of the subject of one of Oscar's lectures, 'Good Taste in House Decor'. There are many descriptions of the house in the various biographies already written, and contemporary comment was coloured by the taste of the beholder. Some regarded it as "bizarre and vaguely sinful", simply because, like Babbacombe Cliff, it was entirely different from any other Victorian residence. H. Montgomery Hyde, in his book *Oscar Wilde*, gives the following description.

Number 16 Tite Street was a four-storey dwelling with a basement. To the right of the entrance hall was a panelled room facing the street, known as the library, which had a strikingly carved wooden mantelpiece and surround to the fireplace. Here Wilde was to do most of his work on a writing-table which had once belonged to Carlyle. The motif of this room was blue and golden brown. On a column in the corner, Wilde placed a plaster cast of the Hermes of Praxiteles, and on the walls he hung a few favourite pictures—a Simeon Solomon, a Monticelli, and a drawing of the actress Mrs. Patrick Campbell by Aubrey Beardsley. To the right of the fireplace there was a large glass-fronted bookcase, full of copies of the Greek classics and other books. Also on the ground floor, leading off the hall at the foot of the staircase and giving on to the garden at the back, was the dining-room; here the prevailing colours were white and grey. The whole of the first floor was taken up by a large drawing-room which was divided in two by folding doors, the front portion above his study being earmarked by Wilde as a smoking-room when the doors were closed. Heavy curtains draped the windows. The walls were lined with a peculiar embossed paper called lincrusta-walton, with a William Morris pattern of dark red and dull gold. The general decor was a mixture of the Far East and Morocco, with divans and a glass bead curtain before the door. A painted grand piano, stood in one corner of the room, occupying a disproportionately large part of it. Opposite the fireplace to the right of the door hung a large painting of Wilde by an American admirer, Harper Pennington. There were two bedrooms on the second floor, and another on the third. The master bedroom, which Oscar and his wife occupied, was the second floor front. Looking out over the back garden, on the third floor was a large room, originally intended as a study for Oscar, but he was to use it seldom, preferring the library on the ground floor for such work as he did at home; it was later to be converted into a day nursery for the two Wilde children.

For the dining-room furniture Godwin designed a suite in white, and also a sideboard, with both of which he took particular pains. The chairs for this room were modelled in various Grecian styles, while round the walls there was a strip of shelving designed to serve for tea parties and buffet suppers—By this arrangement the centre of the room was an open space instead of being absorbed by the customary huge table laden with refreshment, and gave an impression of size and lightness to the room. Another novel feature of the house was that all the doors were removed, except the folding-doors in the drawing-room, and the pictures were protected by curtains.

A contemporary description comes from Adrian Hope, who was shortly to marry Laura Troubridge—he too was not enamoured of Aestheticism.

1885—March 15, I have been lunching with the Oscar Wildes, who both asked to be remembered to you and Amy [Laura's sister]. Through a thick fog I found my way to Tite Street and looked for a white door—which being opened let me into a very ordinary hall passage painted white. Going up a staircase, also white, and covered with a whitish sort of matting, I found the whole of the landing cut off by a dark curtain from the staircase, leaving just room to turn round if you were going higher. I, however, went through the curtain and found rooms to the right and left of the little ante-rooms thus formed. The little man-servant showed me into the room on the left looking out across Tite Street on to the gardens of the Victoria Hospital for Children. No fire and a look as if the furniture had been cleared out for a dance for which the matting did not look inviting. The walls, all white, the ceilings like yours a little [old] but with two lovely dragons painted in the opposite corners of it. On either side of the fireplace, filling up the corners of the room were two three-cornered divans, very low, with cushions, one tiny round Chippendale Table, one arm-chair and three stiff other chairs, also covered with a sort of white lacquer. The arm-chair was a sort of curule chair and very comfy to sit on. This is the summer parlour. Nothing on the walls so as not to break the lines. Certainly a cool-looking room and ought to be seen in the long dog days. Effect on the whole better than it sounds.

All the white paint (as indeed all the paint used about the house) has a high polish like Japanese lacquer work, which has great charm for one who hates paper on walls as much as I do.

The room at the back has a very distinctly Turkish note. No chairs at all. A divan on two sides of the room, very low, with those queer little Eastern inlaid tables in front. A dark dado, but of what colour I know not, as the window, looking on a slum, they have entirely covered with a wooden grating on the inside copied from a Cairo pattern which considerably reduced the little light there was today. A gorgeous ceiling and a fire quite made me fall in love with this room and I thought how lovely someone would look sitting on the divan with her legs crossed and with a faithful slave kissing her pretty bare feet. Here Oscar joined me and presently appeared Constance with her brother and his wife. Lunch was in the dining-room at the back on the ground floor. The room in front they have not as yet fitted up. A cream coloured room with what Oscar assured me, was the only sideboard in England, viz. a board running the whole length of the room and about nine inches wide at the height of the top of the wainscoting. Table of a dirty brown with a strange device: maroon napkins, like some rough bath towels, with deep fringes. Quaint glass and nice food made up a singularly picturesque table. Afterwards we went upstairs to see where the great Oscar sleeps. This room had nothing particular but hers was too delightful. You open the door only to find yourself about to walk through the opening in a wall apparently three feet thick. When you get into the room you find that on the one side of the door, forming a side of the doorway, is an ideal wardrobe with every kind of drawer and hanging cupboard for dresses. Next to this again and between it and the corner of the room is a bookcase and a writing table. All this is white and delightfully clean and fresh besides taking so little room. The writing table is fixed to the bookcase with knee-hole, solid part drawers. The bed looked very soft and nice. Upstairs again Oscar had knocked the garrets into one delightful book room for himself in which he had his bath as well. The doors and woodwork of this room were vermilion with a dado of gold leaves on a vermilion ground giving a delicious effect of colour which I revelled in. Here I sat talking till half-past six and listening to Oscar who, dressed in a grey velvet Norfolk shooting jacket and looking fatter than ever, harangued away in a most amusing way.

His reference to "nice food and a singularly picturesque table" from one so critical was praise indeed. This comment and Constance's articles written for the women's magazines, including the interviews she gave on the subject to the *Ladies' Pictorial* and *To-day* reveal that she was not the inept and bumbling hostess of Frank Harris's imagination.

Laura, in her reply to Adrian's descriptive letter, writes:

> I was so interested in all you told me of the Wildes' house. Some of the new ideas I should think very pretty, I am sure, but I don't think we could live in a room without pictures and books—do you? and all white too and shiny, like living inside a jam-pot—without the jam! But I should like the Turkish room the best—for very idle times! Her room sounds charming and the whole thing is not nearly so fantastic and outré as one would expect, evidently. You do not say if Mrs. Oscar was dressed to live up to her husband's lectures or was she still swathed in a limp white muslin and lilies? But it must have been amusing altogether.

That Constance had a reputation among her staid and prim relatives for being Aesthetic is borne out by Laura's reference to her room being "not nearly so fantastic and outré as one would expect". In making fun of Constance's clothes, Laura notes Adrian's lack of reportage on the subject by asking if she was living up to Oscar's lectures. Comment like this gives the impression that all her clothes were designed by her husband, which was of course not true. A woman of so independent a spirit would not have tolerated such dominance. Before her marriage her clothes were so striking that, as she and Oscar strolled about Chelsea, an urchin remarked, " 'Amlet and Ophelia out for a walk I suppose," to which Oscar replied, "My little fellow, you are quite right, we are." Being an ardent Pre-Raphaelite, Constance was quite at home in her muslin drapes and floppy hats—perhaps Laura wished she had the courage to be so trendy.

In the year 1885, twelve months after Jimmy Whistler's Sunday morning breakfast party, Constance became the 'Chatelaine of the House Beautiful'. One can imagine her as she wandered about in a pale green robe, sampling the newness and treading as if on virgin snow, marvelling at the expensive simplicity, revelling in the revolutionary white walls and the lightness, the airiness. It was not anything like Ely Place, or Lancaster Gate, Devonshire Terrace or Sussex Gardens where she had been brought up. The artistic elegance would be pleasing and all of it individual and redolent of memory, such as the bronze overmantel executed by "Donaghue, of the handsome Roman face with the Irish blue eyes". The scene was from the poem 'Requiescat', in memory of Oscar's little sister. Did she hope that the coming baby would be a girl? Her imagination must have run to the family they would raise here, dolls perched on the sideboard, boys sprawling on the Japanese sofa, for this was to be the Merrion Square kind of house where it would not be thought improper for children to mix with grown-ups in the drawing-rooms.

Her own personal objects had settled into the premises as though they too had come home: her treasured pieces of small furniture, the French writing-table and chair, the Venetian glass vases on the ivory inlaid card table, the William Morris rug, miniatures given to her by Edward Burne-Jones, the picture from John Ruskin, the travelling bookcase which housed her precious Keats and Tasso.

In order to run the four-storeyed house, plus basement and attics, Constance engaged a cook, a housemaid who lived out and a butler of outstanding merit by the name of Arthur. He was small, mild-natured and briskly capable, and he lived-in.

As for Oscar, she found him more tender than she had dreamed: considerate and ardent in a hundred happy ways; not the deliverer of "*bons mots* between mouthfuls", not the young blade of the *Patience* tour, but her Oscar, who laughed softly and sang out of tune, and absently caressed the lobe of his ear when absorbed in a book.

Out of the many beautiful things which were showered upon their house-warming, Constance treasured most a crimson leather-bound autograph or visitor's book, and on the first page Oscar had written, in his impeccably styled handwriting, one of his poems, prophetic almost—entitled simply, 'To My Wife'.

> I can write no stately proem
> as a prelude to my lay;
> From a poet to a poem
> I would dare to say
>
> For if of these fallen petals
> One to you seem fair;
> Love will waft it till it settles,
> On your hair.

And when wind and winter harden
All the loveless land,
It will whisper of the garden,
You will understand.

7

The House Beautiful

Residing in the House Beautiful did not ease the Wildes' financial burden, for, in sending off a cheque in payment for Edward Godwin's furniture, Oscar laments his inability to finance an extension to the premises for which a plan had been drawn up. There was also the added expense of providing for the coming baby, but shortage of money was not allowed to cramp their life-style, and modifications and additions to the existing décor were put in hand.

Although six months pregnant, Constance, after the manner of some Victorian women, did not shun the social scene, for she took a box at the Lyceum Theatre for herself and friends to attend after dinner. It was about this time, too, that she went on the stage, being one of the Greek chorus who, in white robes, "absolutely stilled the audience" by their sinuous procession. One of the dramatic reviews had this to say: "Helen in Troas is a lavish spectacular set in a circus of an arena to show off the fine props of the Greek chorus against a brilliant background of scenery and costume. Among many female beauties in the large cast was Constance Wilde who was one of Helen's hand maidens." It says much for her looks that she was singled out for praise.

As man cannot live by poems alone, Oscar decided it was high time to subsidize his artistic inclinations by seeking steady, but remunerative, employment of the nine-to-five variety.

The reason for wanting work emerged on the morning of 5th June, in the form of a son, Cyril. The yellow and dove-grey staircase echoed to Cyril's lusty wails, and his parents were ecstatic. Only one godparent was appointed—an odd choice—a young man called Walter Harris, a friend of Constance and later a crony of the Ranee. It was an odd choice in the respect of his becoming a Moslem and taking up residence in Tangier. Still, the Wildes were anything but conventional. Among a welter of telegrams, Oscar urged all his friends to marry at once; those already married were urged to become parents, and those already with a family urged to increase it. Cyril was a strong, healthy baby, and Constance recovered quickly from the birth. A resident nurse was employed to look after the little fellow, and the large bedroom to the back of the second floor was fitted out as a nursery. He also wrote to Edward Heron Allen asking him to draw up a horoscope for their son. It was beautifully designed and detailed; the boy was to grow handsome and strong, and although they did not believe it, he was according to the horoscope destined for a military career, all of which came true. Oscar was not the only one to write about his son. Adrian Hope on 8th June wrote to his fiancée: "Did you see the Wildes have a boy, I rather pity the infant don't you?" To which she replied, with great alacrity, "I had not heard of the arrival of the infant Wilde—I agree that it is much to be pitied. Will it be swathed in artistic baby clothes? Sage green bibs and tuckers, I suppose, and a peacock blue robe." But the ecstatic Wildes were impervious to comment.

As nothing had yet materialized in the way of employment, Oscar continued to contribute articles to a variety of magazines and still delivered the odd lecture. By the spring of 1886, when Cyril—who was called by his paternal grandma "the little prince"—was nine months old, Constance was pregnant again. They hoped for a daughter this time and planned to call her Isola Deirdre. What Constance's family thought of such a short interval between children can be imagined, but Lady Wilde was so overjoyed that she installed a large rocking-horse in readiness to accommodate her grandchildren.

Constance visited her mother-in-law regularly; they sometimes went shopping together, and she regularly passed on her copy of the *Ladies' Pictorial*. Constance had always been in the confidence of Lady Wilde, who called on her to cash cheques and even borrow the odd sovereign—all, one can be sure, faithfully repaid. Lady Wilde also had news: Park Street, where she lived, was due to be developed as a shopping area. She was at first quite indignant about it but consoled herself by moving to Chelsea, which was a much more artistic quarter, and where she planned to hold a salon. She could have had a rival in the form of Mrs Ronalds, mistress of composer Arthur Sullivan, who lived in an elaborate establishment in nearby Cadogan Square. But, neither lady had a wish to compete, and they held their salons on different days.

So 'Speranza' moved to 146 Oakley Street. In those days it was a wide thoroughfare sweeping down to the river, with solid, ivy-clad houses, and where solid, dignified citizens parted their curtains hurriedly at the clatter of so many hansom cabs shattering their Sunday peace, to stare in amazement at the literati who crowded her receptions.

Constance and Oscar attended whenever they could, for 'holding court' was life itself to 'Speranza' of the Irish Nationalists. Dressed, or overdressed as was usually the case, she created her own theatrical atmosphere by drawing the blinds and lighting her rooms with the soft glow of candlelight, introducing people with whispered explanations of their characteristics. Here, on Sunday mornings, she relived her Dublin days and indulged her fantasies to the full. Especially was she thrilled when Americans steamed up the Thames to attend her gatherings. "All London comes to me by way of King's Road," she declared, "but the Americans come straight from the Atlantic steamers moored at Chelsea Bridge!"

The weeks and months of Constance's radiant existence in that year of 1886 were overshadowed by the news of Nellie, her sister-in-law, petitioning for a divorce from Otho. They had only been married as long as the Wildes and, living in London, had often called at Tite Street; there were no children of the marriage. The divorce action and record seem to have faded into obscurity, but of course not all actions were reported even when divorce was rare.

In 1886 a wife could obtain a divorce from her husband on the grounds of incest, bigamy, rape, sodomy, bestiality, cruelty coupled with adultery, or adultery coupled with desertion without lawful excuse for two years. Seeing that there was no desertion, and certainly no incest, bigamy, sodomy or bestiality (such would have at least interested the newspapers), there is only rape or cruelty coupled with adultery left. Perhaps the Holland temper had been rearing its ugly head. What a shock for the family—for Aunt Carrie, whose favourite he was and who had given a party in his honour, and for his mother and Mr King. Scandal of one kind or another never seemed far away from the Lloyds and Wildes. Whatever the cause of Otho's divorce, it carried stigma enough for him to change his names about and use his middle name as surname, to be known as Otho Holland, and then to go into voluntary exile on the Continent for twenty years or so, returning to end his days in Bournemouth, where he died as a result of a fall in the black-out in 1943.

Oscar, having survived fatherhood for the first time, although considerate and attentive, was no longer in the first flush of wonder at the prospect of the event due in November. He was more in demand socially, and if there were early squalls on the matrimonial sea, they would be more evident in this last month, when Constance, due to bad weather and her condition, would not be able to accompany him.

Such a situation was not peculiar to the Wildes alone; it has had its counterpart many times before and since. Some biographers say that she was "insanely jealous"—as her story unfolds, it would seem that the word "insanely" was going a bit far—but given these circumstances, it was most likely that the expectant mother sat at home imagining her husband charming his hostess and her guests with that beautifully modulated voice; standing, with cigarette in hand, head slightly to one side, his lips pouting with humorous hesitation as though suspending judgement on some amusing story—by now she would be familiar with his repertoire, his gestures; and if her brother had committed adultery, she could be forgiven for entertaining the slightest suspicion that Oscar could be on the same track. But then he would be back, massive in fur coat, cane and hat still in hand, breathless from a recent attack of asthma, his clothes smelling of fog and cigars. Their moments of reconciliation were searing matters of the soul, where their tears would fall together. He was an emotional man, easily moved and of a deep sensitivity, and in some respects very much like the father she had adored.

Isola Deirdre turned out to be Vyvyan Oscar Beresford Wilde. Their second son was born about 3rd November. Each parent thought the other had registered the birth, and by the time the error was discovered, neither could recall the actual date! Constance wrote to John Ruskin, her Pre-Raphaelite hero, asking him to be the child's godparent, but he declined on account of his age. Vyvyan therefore had to be content with Mortimer Mempis, artist, dandy and Pre-

Raphaelite.

No sooner was Constance in circulation again than the business of life and social engagements came down on them heavily in the form of Mrs Cooper Oakley, who was about to open the first West End restaurant for working girls and needed social luminaries for good publicity and a sensational opening. Constance's full-skirted velvet coat, cut on the dashing style of a highwayman's coat, received as much comment as Lady Hope's furs. All the fashionable ladies were there: the Honourable Mrs Bevan, the Countess of Wachtesmiester and the Honourable Mrs Borthwick. They chatted to Lady Dorothy Neville, for whom Constance did not care, and Lady Colin Campbell, for whom Oscar did not care, and people for whom they both did not care. After the luncheon, when coffee was served and cigarettes lit, Madam Blavatsky, whom Oscar had met at the Theosophical Dinner, disapproved in a loud voice both of mesmerism and of Mrs Annie Besant, who was attracting the attention of the Press on account of her "militant costume" and pamphlets on birth control. Mrs Cooper Oakley must have been grateful when Oscar took Madam in hand and edged her on to amuse them all, amicably, in spirited conversation with himself on the relative merits of Theosophy and Aestheticism. They were not the only ones to be amused: the Press reports that "The lower classes who had gathered outside, now pressed their faces to the windows to remark on the antics of society—and the spectacle of ladies smoking, in particular."

The year of Vyvyan's birth was quite sensational in a local way. The Ranee of Sarawak's brother, Harry de Windt, performed the—for then—most remarkable feat of travelling to Peking from Paris overland. Frank Miles, the artist, the hybridizer of lilies and one-time friend of Oscar's, was committed to an asylum for the insane. In May Oscar's first long story, 'Lord Arthur Saville's Crime', was published in the *Court and Society Review*. Things were looking up. Cassells, the publishers, appointed Oscar the editor of *Ladies' World*, a fashionable magazine, which he renamed *Women's World* at the request of female militants.

The new editor upped the sales at once and even audaciously asked Queen Victoria to contribute! The famous, the artistic, the academic, the militant—all brands of women's interests were catered for. Lady Wilde provided Irish poems, and Adrian Hope was impressed enough to sound Oscar out about Laura's doing some drawing for it—"if there is any money in the project". The editor was non-committal, and Laura was never asked to contribute. Constance wrote some interesting articles for the magazine, including one which was a good specimen of the museum-made article, on the history of muffs. Men, it revealed, first sported the muff in 1600: there is an illustration of Admiral Byng with sword at his side and a huge fur muff on his left arm. King Charles's spaniels were carried about in them; and a Spaniard earned for himself the distinction of suspending his muff from a cord about his neck! Eccentric muffs abounded, such as those made of Angora wool which trailed on the ground.

More original was the article on Constance's pet subject of clothes, children's this time. It illustrates her interest in healthy clothing and dress reform and deplores the dressing-up of children to resemble miniature adults. She advocates Turkish trousers for girls and what we would call a 'jump suit'. A duffle coat is illustrated, and the accent is on warmth and freedom of movement. Knitted jerseys with shorts and stockings to match were the 'in' thing for small boys. There is a delightful portrait of Cyril wearing one of these suits. "I am glad," she writes, "that plush is giving place to rough clothes for children's outdoor dress . . . it seems scarcely suitable for the free physical life that is absolutely necessary to a healthy child." The article ends with a plea: "The Rational Dress should be adopted by all mothers who wish their girls to grow up healthy and happy." Part of this consisted of "woollen stays, to button not to lace . . . a divided skirt and smock overall". She concludes: "There are many little girls who wear this dress now and I hope to see the number largely increased year by year."

The coverage of Irving's Benefit in July that year (1889) illustrates the lightness of her style:

At the Play. The Lyceum: Saturday Night. The season is at an end, the curtain has fallen upon the familiar last scene of The Merchant of Venice, the last bouquets of the season have been showered across the footlights, and that popular speaker, Mr. Henry Irving, has delivered his valedictory address. The stalls and boxes were full of familiar faces, the pit and gallery were crowded with old friends and hearty admirers, and a tremendous burst of applause naturally greeted the appearance of the popular actor-manager, who having exchanged the Jewish gaberdine of Shylock for evening dress of the Victorian era, came before the curtain to receive the parting congratulations of the assembled audience. The speech was a characteristic one—playful, yet earnest, and enlivened with many sly touches of quaint satiric humour. He spoke of the phenomenal success which had attended the run of Faust, which, produced in 1885, has continued its career with undiminished éclat until the close of the present season of 1887. The devil's own luck, some people might call it, said Mr. Irving; but for his own part he preferred to think that 'Needs must, when the devil drives.' Invitations to represent Faust in many of the great European capitals had reached the managerial headquarters, and the successful production of the play had been specially gratifying to all real lovers of Goethe, in that it had been the means of multiplying his English readers by tens of thousands, and of increasing the foreign sale of his works to an extraordinary extent. Enterprising advertisers also had availed themselves of the popular enthusiasm for Faust to impress upon the blank spaces between the pages of the play recommendatory paragraphs recounting their wares, and chaste designs illustrative of the Margarets hoe, the Mephistopheles hat, and other appropriately-named articles. Even Beecham, the immortal inventor of the pill that bore his name, had endeavoured to turn the thoughts of the many readers of the play from poetry to prosaic medicine, by informing them that the price of the infallible remedy was one and three-halfpence a box, and that it could only be purchased under a Government stamp, and from a licensed vendor. He than spoke of Werner and The Amber Heart, both of which would again be presented upon the Lyceum stage on the return of the company to England, and, with a gracefully-expressed compliment to Mdme. Sarah Bernhardt and a hearty wish of success to Miss Anderson, whose season at the Lyceum commences in September next, ended by bidding all his friends in front, in the name of himself, of Miss Ellen Terry, and the whole of the company, not farewell, but au revoir. In addition to the truly marvellous production of the Merchant of Venice, a most charming supper party was given afterwards on the stage, where there were assembled a great number of pretty and interesting people. Miss Ellen Terry appeared first in her terra-cotta Venetian dress, and afterwards in a soft white woollen costume embroidered in Oriental colourings. Her daughter, an interesting-looking girl, though absolutely unlike her mother, wore dark coral pink. Mrs. Bram Stoker wore white satin. Mrs. Savile Clarke wore dark bronze cotton crepe embroidered with a surface pattern of gold, while her younger children wore their 'Alice in Wonderland' dresses, and looked very pretty. The palm of beauty was perhaps borne off by Mrs. Weldon, radiant and young-looking as ever. Mr. Toole, Colonel Cody, Mr. and Mrs. Burnand, Mrs. Louise Chandler Moulton, Mr. and Mrs. Beatty-Kingston, Miss Bessie Hatton, Mrs. Terry, Mrs. Arthur Lewis, Miss Marion Terry, Mr. and Mrs. George Alexander, Dr. Quain, Mr. and Mrs. Stephen Coleridge, Mr. and Mrs. Oscar Wilde, and Mr. and Mrs. Comyns Carr were among the guests present. There were many children, Mr. Goodhall's little daughter and niece amongst them. Last, but not least, among the guests must be mentioned Mr. Irving's fox terrier Fussy, who found many old friends and new admirers.

The said Mrs Weldon thought that Oscar had written the report and wrote to thank him for it—he replied with thanks, saying that the credit must go to his wife.

Constance always had faith in her husband; she believed him to be a genius and consequently, unknown to him, sent 'Lord Arthur Saville's Crime' off to America, to her friend Eddie Heron Allen, who was visiting the States, and asked him to see if McClures would buy it.

The family on both sides of the Irish Sea no doubt heaved a sigh of relief that Constance's husband had at last contrived to seek some 'honourable employment', but knowing him, she must have wondered as she saw him off to the office, dressed in the part of a city editor, how long it would be before he tired of so mundane a routine.

During these early years of marriage, the Wildes wandered amongst an intellectual group nicknamed 'the Souls', who were as interested in Liberal politics as in literature and exceedingly good taste. The brilliant Margot Tennant, who was later to become the second Mrs Asquith, and Arthur Balfour, hellenist, politician, lover of music, player of tennis, were just two of the distinguished names. Constance, moving in this élite circle, could hardly have been as shy and tongue-tied as the early biographers make out. 'The Souls' did not suffer fools at all—let alone gladly. And Constance knew Arthur Balfour well enough to appeal to him later, on her husband's behalf. It is said that at these gatherings, 'The pretty women ran after Oscar and allowed him great familiarities, although there was no question of love making." As Constance did not regularly accompany her husband, it would seem she was not "insanely jealous" or she would have been on guard; besides, as a beautiful woman, she would not have lacked masculine attention herself.

The year following Vyvyan's birth was sensational in another respect, the import of which Constance—and even Oscar—could not in the wildest flight of imagination have grasped. The Wildes were introduced by an artist friend to Mrs Ross, widow of a Canadian Attorney-General, and her sons, Alec, secretary to the Society of Authors, and twenty-year-old Robbie, who was interested in Art Criticism. The latter and Oscar were to become close friends, but in 1887 Robbie Ross was awaiting entrance to Cambridge University and was paying-guest at 16 Tite Street for two months while his mother wintered abroad. He was not a good-looking young man, but his delightful nature offset his turned-up nose and convex forehead. Already the young Robbie was possessed of amazing conversational qualities and wit. He was also homosexual. As yet, Oscar was not.

Constance was used to the clusters of literary-aspiring young men who regarded the House Beautiful as a shrine, and who were collectively nicknamed 'the disciples', and as far as she was concerned, young Ross was just another.

While Robbie was at King's College, Oscar continued his daily stint at the office and had published *The Happy Prince and other Tales*, which did not sell very well. Meanwhile, back with the family, Constance's brother Otho surprised them all by marrying again. Nellie, his ex-wife, followed suit by marrying a Swiss doctor by the name of Grandjean—and they all lived happily ever after. Not forgetting Laura Troubridge—she married her Adrian, becoming Mrs Hope, and took a house further along Tite Street. Willie Wilde was trying his best not to follow suit. He was being pursued ardently by a rich American widow—Mrs Leslie of *Leslie's Illustrated News*—on the look-out for a fourth husband. She was twenty years older than Willie, a woman of mystery of whom it was said that her mother had kept a brothel. She was a mulatto, and an energetic one at that, for her third husband, Frank Leslie, under her pressure had established seven newspapers in America; perhaps, seeing that Willie was a journalist, she had further hopes in this direction.

In October Grandmama Atkinson died. Constance accompanied her mother to the funeral in Dublin, leaving the children with their nurse and Oscar. It was her last visit. The heads of both the English and the Irish families were gone. It was the end of an era. 'Mama Mary', as Mrs Atkinson was called by the Lloyd children, had told them exciting little stories, which the following year Constance wrote up into a children's book, called *There was Once*. It contained coloured illustrations and was published both in Britain and in America.

Constance had been interested in Theosophy ever since it had hit town some few years since, and early in 1888 she joined the Order of the Golden Dawn, which was a kind of Neoplatonist and cabbalistic mysticism expressed in Buddhist terminology. Another person joined the order about the same time, a silly, rich American woman called the Comtesse de Brémont. She was a singer and journalist who came to her French title by marrying into it in New York. She was a hanger-on at Lady Wilde's soirées and wrote in 1911 the most absurd of all the many books about Oscar Wilde; she is said to have died in London in 1922. What concerns the present biography is her outrageous attitude to Constance Wilde, such as "having to take her by the hand to join . . . she was so timid and afraid", and then the Comtesse proceeds to further the outrage by stating that Constance was asked to leave because she had not the intelligence to follow the teaching. Nothing could have been further from the truth. Firstly, they did not join together, and according to the records of the Order, Constance by the following November had reached the Senior Philosopher's Grade— quite an achievement; it was the Comtesse who had been asked to leave, not Constance.

Readers of Wilde's biographies will be familiar with such deprecating comments which have been sanctified by long repetition and accepted without question by successive biographers. They are too numerous to be dealt with in their abounding entirety, but, seeing that this work is of a vindicatory nature, one more instance will suffice. Even the clever and distinguished Philippe Jullian repeats the, by now, legendary phrase: "Constance consoled herself for having to lead a so-called brilliant life by the company of Margaret, Lady Sandhurst, who was a zealous worker for the Church." Others refer to the "staunchly evangelical Constance".

Lady Sandhurst was certainly a zealous worker, but not for the Church. She was President of the Women's Liberal Federation of which Constance was a member. The Federation aimed at quickening the interest of women in politics and the emancipation of their sex. Both she and Constance supported and worked for Women's Suffrage. Lady Sandhurst was a persuasive and accomplished platform speaker who addressed—without the aid of notes—thirty-six great audiences in three months. One open-air meeting attracted a crowd of ten thousand. No matter how busy, she never refused an invitation from any of the women's associations. Apart from being an earnest advocate of Women's Suffrage and Home Rule for Ireland— her husband having been in charge of the forces there—she had four sons and a daughter about Constance's age. (The eldest son married Earl Spencer's sister.) This stately woman, mobile of face, her dark hair drawn back from a wide forehead, started the 'Lady Sandhurst Children's Home' in the Marylebone Road. It was not the usual philanthropic venture for waifs and strays but came about as a result of a relative of hers being remarkably cured by 'a massage treatment', which convinced her of the efficacy of manipulative healing. The same treatment was given to children who were stunted in growth or diseased and deformed in limb, with amazing results. This then was Constance's friend. One of her militant lectures appears in a copy of *Women's World*, which Oscar was editing. Her ladyship died in 1892 aged sixty-four. As for Constance's church connections, there was a wide gulf fixed between Anglican Evangelicalism and the tenets of the Golden Dawn movement. Evidence points to both the Wildes attending church only out of politeness when visiting people who did. The older Constance grew, the more she fancied the Roman Catholic Church, but, unlike Oscar, she was never received into it. The other views and comments which water Constance's character down to the banal and ineffectual originated from the biased and prejudiced view of Oscar's homosexual friends.

One of these friends, the young Robbie Ross, was the unfortunate victim in March 1889 of an incident which cut short his university career. He was ducked in the fountain at King's, "to drown his Aesthetic affectations", and became very ill as a result. Consequently, he did not return but turned to journalism and art criticism in London.

In July four-year-old Cyril was very ill. It was the first serious illness, and his parents were very worried. Imagine Constance's concern to hear that, despite his anxiety, Oscar was due to dine with Oscar Browning, don of Cambridge, and Robbie Ross. Both little boys adored their father, and the nursery, a scene of great hilarity when he was there, was now silent, the gas turned down, the boy fretful.

Although Oscar was always a loving and indulgent parent, he would most likely have attended the dinner engagement if Constance had not put her foot down and insisted he stayed. The introduction of Ross's name into the Wilde saga does not mean he was necessarily Oscar's first lover, although many years later he stated that he was. It is not the purpose of this book to delve into the who's who of Wilde's relationships, or to present opinions to prove or disprove their validity. Ross may well have been the first serious male friend—and as such presented a threat to Constance—he was certainly the most devoted, being with Wilde to the end of his life and eventually his literary executor. Of all her husband's friends, Constance appeared, in the long term, to like and trust Ross, but in the short term she was naturally impatient of his keeping Oscar from Carlyle's writing-table. After Cyril had improved, the appointment with Ross was of course kept, and it introduced shadows into a relationship which had been, mainly, five years of sunshine.

Cyril's illness proved to be a bad dose of the measles. The rash eventually faded, but the same could not be said for Robbie Ross; his presence was to be with the Wildes for a long time.

This year was the watershed as far as the Wildes' marriage was concerned—from that date on, it began to trickle downhill. Constance had held the stage and been the centre of it for five years; she was now being slightly eased toward the wings, in order to make room for someone else.

When her husband started coming home not merely in the 'early hours'—which was the usual thing for the socially artistic man-about-town—but at dawn, Constance, like countless other wives before and since, must have wondered what occupied him and the disciples. Gambling? Drinking? Women? Eventually the time came when he no longer shared her bed but kept to his own room—no doubt making these 'unsocial hours' an excuse, not to disturb her. Because Constance was still very much in love with her husband, she spent many a sleepless night wondering why he was avoiding making love to her. It was not that they were unsatisfied with each other; sex had brought fulfilment to both. She would consider that there was nothing more degrading and futile than a failed marriage. There had been a lot of it about. Take her own parents for instance . . . Sir William Wilde . . . brother Willie and his womanizing . . . Otho. She may have even wondered if marital infidelity was inherited! Lady Colin Campbell had recently given the Press a whirl with her divorce proceedings, and to Constance, lying awake and alone at night, it would seem as if her marriage was going the same way. Hardest of all to bear was that Oscar, who was so sensitive, whose emotions could quiver with perception, could treat her in so insensitive a manner.

Did Constance, with some apprehension, tackle him about his growing indifference, or did he come to her with his tale of woe? The author agrees with Mr Montgomery Hyde that it was the resurgence of syphilis, contracted in his Oxford days, which suspended their relations.

Some writers have held the view that Constance never knew of the outbreak of syphilis and thought he had ceased to find her sexually attractive because of other women. Considering the passionate nature behind her Pre-Raphaelite façade, and the Holland temper lurking in the background, it would be more in keeping with such a character to insist on knowing—and after all, she had every right to know why he no longer made love to her. She was a determined woman when roused—remember her attitude toward the London family whom she thought might oppose her engagement. That she should be informed of the eruption of the disease is not so bizarre a notion, and Oscar could have voluntarily told her. But it is more than likely that he, who was ever the unconventional, the outspoken, on subjects taboo, hedged about in the hope of an early cure, in which case she would never know the sordid facts. Besides, there was in Wilde the desire to dice with destruction, deliberately to cast himself down to see what the gods cast up. He took a chance, and one can be certain that he would be really penitent, filled with a soul-searing remorse for the sins of his youth. Constance would see through a mist of tears in those almond-shaped eyes shame, sorrow, remorse and sadness for the burden he had laid upon her. He was to say on future occasions of penitence, "I who would give you the world seem destined to bring you nothing but unhappiness."

Even though the revelation may have filled her with a kind of horror, it was tinged with relief that there was no 'other woman' and that he had not grown indifferent. He had cast himself down, most likely at her knees, and found the gods, or in this case Constance, kind. He had received absolution from the hands of his priestess. It had been in his best interests to clear the air, for if he had not, there would have been scenes and recriminations, and in the end Constance would have worn him down and winkled the awful truth out of him. Any honourable man in Victoria's age would have felt deeply ashamed—more so Oscar, for he knew that his wife worshipped him, and in one blow it had been revealed that her god's feet were made of clay. Having smoothed matters over on his domestic front, he could now turn his attention to dear Robbie.

As for Constance, when the shock had worn off, there would build up a natural resentment that his past pilgrimages to the haunts of pleasure should deprive her of the love which was her legal right and which she so much desired. But after all, he had put her welfare and that of any future children first. Some men would have said nothing. Did she shudder to recall Ibsen's play *Ghosts*, which they had seen on the London stage? A play of which venereal disease was the theme, where the sins of the father were visited upon the son.

About this time Constance stayed for a few weeks in the summer with her friend Emily Thursfield, reviewer for the *Guardian*, in a rented rectory on the Yorkshire moors. Could it have been a retreat to come to terms with the revelation or to recuperate from the shock?

All things pass, and life would eventually assume more natural proportions, but Oscar's confession, apart from adding a gravity to Constance's life which had not been there before, enabled her to view her husband with an objectivity impossible before. Perhaps this was the first questioning, the first inkling of shadowy places in his life—questioning, such as how could the youthful Apostle of Aestheticism, so appreciative of the fair and beautiful, have wallowed in the depravity of brothels. André Raffalovich remembers Constance Wilde saying, "Oscar likes you so much—that you have such nice improper talks together."

Oscar was always attentive, and he went out of his way to pay her extra little attentions, which he knew would make her feel like a goddess; for, come Robbie, come syphylis, come whatever, although he had got over being riotously in love with his wife, he was still very fond of her, and it was part of his outgoing nature to show it.

Constance had, apart from her own income which afforded independence, a wide circle of friends and varied interests, which was a good thing in view of her husband's ever-widening activities. She, as well as Oscar, spent time away from home and children, for Cyril and Vyvyan were well catered for in the hands of their nurse and doting aunts, although the Wildes tried to make sure that one parent was in residence if the other was away. Wilde was a kind and indulgent father, and in her absence Constance knew they would be safe and happy with him. Possessing so imaginative a parent was the passport to new and exciting games. Toys would suddenly be embellished with powers hitherto unknown; nursery animals waxed eloquent; scarlet-coated soldiers lined up for battle. Being an unusually natural creature—when with his family—he was very much at ease with children. He mended their big wooden fort when repeated battles had proved too much for it, and, when the occasion demanded (no doubt that was often), he engaged in a rough-and-tumble with real enthusiasm, giving piggy-backs, going down on hands and knees to be climbed over. Nor were they always confined to the first-floor nursery: he sometimes took his sons to play in the dining-room by way of special concession, where Edward Godwin's expensive white dining-suite with its Grecian chairs came in for all kinds of improvisation.

Richard le Gallienne relates this charming story of an afternoon tea with the Wildes after which, while *en famille* in the drawing-room, and indicating Cyril, Wilde said:

It is the duty of every father to write fairy tales for his children. But the mind of a child is a great mystery. It is incalculable and who shall divine it, or bring to it its own peculiar delights? You humbly spread before it the treasures of your imagination, and they are but dross. For example, a day or two ago, Cyril yonder came to me with the question, "Father, do you ever dream?" "Why of course, my darling. It is the first duty of a gentleman to dream." "And what do you dream of?" asked Cyril, with a child's disgusting appetite for facts. Then I, believing, of course, that something picturesque was expected of me, spoke of magnificent things: "What do I dream of? Oh, I dream of dragons with gold and silver scales, and scarlet flames coming out of their mouths, of eagles with eyes made of diamonds that can see over the whole world at once, of lions with yellow manes, and voices like thunder, of elephants with little houses on their backs, and tigers and zebras with barred and spotted coats . . ." So I laboured on with my fancy, till, observing that Cyril was entirely unimpressed, and indeed, quite undisguisedly bored, I came to a humiliating stop, and, turning to my son, there, I said: "But tell me, what do you dream of, Cyril?" His answer was like a divine revelation: "I dream of pigs," he said.

Herbert Vivian wrote:

The two characters in Wilde's article 'The Decay of Lying' he told me, were named after his own two little boys, to their no small delight. Some of his anecdotes about these children were amusing. "I plaster the walls of their rooms," he said, "with texts about early rising and sluggards and so forth, and I tell them that, when they grow up, they must take their father as a warning, and occasionally have breakfast earlier than two in the afternoon." Cyril, not yet five, bewildered his family one morning by announcing that he did not mean to say his prayers any more. It was pointed out to him that he must pray God to make him good, but he demurred that he did not want to be made good and was not going to pray for what he did not want. Papa Oscar persevered for a long time without making the faintest impression, but he felt more than rewarded for all his efforts, when after a protracted altercation, the young philosopher offered a compromise, and said he wouldn't mind praying God to make his baby brother good! Oscar moralized delightfully over this and said it was human nature all over. We were all anxious to have other people made good, provided we were not troubled ourselves, only we had not the candour to say so!

Apart from the usual social whirl of seasonal concerts, operas, theatres, attending lectures and that all-important Victorian institution called 'visiting', there is ample evidence of the busy life Constance led. With Oscar, she was a member of the Albemarle Club, founded in 1881 at a cost of eight guineas to join and five per annum, "Where ladies can entertain friends of both sexes, or pleasantly pass the time of day with the papers".

Her regular attendance at the meetings of the Pre-Raphaelite Society began before she met Oscar and continued long after her husband's interest in "civilising the provinces" had faded. (The manager of Hatchard's bookshop in Piccadilly and also Hatchard himself were also members.) Her interest in the Order of the Golden Dawn has given rise to many references to "Constance took refuge in spiritualism" or "She became a spiritualist". That she and Oscar were superstitious is borne out by their visits to the fashionable fortune-teller Mrs Robinson, but of addiction to séances and spiritualism there is no evidence.

Come election time Constance did her share, with Lady Sandhurst, of canvassing for the Liberal candidate. The cause of the Rational Dress Society and its gazette, which she was editing, was absorbing. The paper's circulation was among a mere five hundred—there was much to be done in recruiting advertisers, obtaining good names to write equally good articles, persuading popular speakers, of whom she was one herself, to address meetings. At one stage she had doubts of honouring a promise of one such speech due to being over-involved. She organized concerts and fund-raising events, taking advantage of her position to badger the arty and literati to give of their services in various good causes.

Then there were the Embroidery Guilds with May Morris—daughter of William; and her 'At Home', which was held on Thursday afternoons and filled her crimson leather visitor's book with interesting names. Also, there were bazaars and fêtes, for this was the age of the bazaar, and well-known names—Constance being one—were in demand to boost the product. An accomplished pianist herself, she took time off to attend musical weekends. On a visit to the Isle of Wight her mother-in-law asked her to look up Lady Meath to find out if she visited the Queen at Osborne, 'Speranza's' interest being to enlist the aid of the Meaths—near neighbours when in Ireland—to put in a word for a civil pension, which, through his lordship, was eventually obtained.

Frequent visits were made to Lady Mount Temple—her beloved 'Mia Madre'—at Babbacombe Cliff, and to the novelist George

Meredith and his family, with whom she was well acquainted; there were Easter parties with the Burne-Joneses and the Walter Palmers at Frognall; these latter two were also family affairs which the children loved, on account of the biscuit factory owned by the Palmers— Huntley & Palmer—and occasionally being taken to see it and, what was even better, taste freshly baked samples.

Despite the Wildes' domestic problem, marriage was flourishing elsewhere. The golden-haired darling of Monegasque Society, Constance's friend Alice, had married His Serene Highness Prince Albert of Monaco and consequently become a Serene Highness herself. Willie Wilde had at last gracefully succumbed to the attention of the wealthy Mrs Leslie and to everyone's relief had been whisked away to America and honourable matrimony. "God keep them happy and wise, and living in truth and trust," Lady Wilde wrote hopefully. "I think her influence must work in him, and give him the strength he needs."

Oscar, by now, had lost interest in, and given up, the editorship of *Women's World*, for he was on the threshold of literary success. Apart from poems, essays and articles, *The Happy Prince and other Tales* had been published in 1888, followed by *The Portrait of Mr. W.H.*, a theory about Shakespeare's 'dark lady'—who turns out not to be a lady, after all! Success would come much sooner, Constance often said, if Robbie Ross and the other disciples would leave him alone to work. But success came quickly enough, for in June 1890 *Lippincote's Magazine* published 'The Picture of Dorian Gray', which played havoc with Victorian susceptibilities. The newspapers panned it. The *Daily Chronicle* wrote: "Dullness and dirt are the chief features of Lippincoates magazine this month. The unclean element in it, though undeniably amusing, is Mr. Oscar Wilde's story. . . . It is spawned from the leprous literature of the French Decadents, a poisonous book, the atmosphere of which is heavy with mephitic odours of moral and spiritual putrefaction. . . ." The *Scots Observer* was even worse. "Mr. Wilde," their review went, "has brains and art, and style, but if he can write for none but outlawed noblemen and perverted telegraph boys, the sooner he takes to tailoring or some other decent trade, the better. . . ."

The "outlawed nobleman and perverted telegraph boys" was a reference to a fearful scandal which had been given tremendous publicity. The scandal was uncovered when a male brothel, whose speciality was telegraph boys, was raided in Cleveland Street; of the people charged, only a clergyman and a clerk were arrested and consequently imprisoned for 'Acts of Impropriety'. The Press had been suspicious of a 'hush-up', for several noblemen had also been involved, two of whom were consequently named. One was Lord Arthur Somerset, nicknamed 'Podge', son of the Duke of Beaufort, an ex-Guards Officer who managed the Prince of Wales's racing stables. He fled the country, but, outlawed as he was, it was rumoured that he returned regularly to see his parents. Out of the enquiry into the 'hush-up' came coverage of further scandal, in the *Eustace* v *Parke* libel, the former being Lord Eustace, the second nobleman involved.

Such a Philistine reaction stung Oscar to defend 'Dorian' in a letter to the Press, in which he maintained that the story would be ultimately recognized for what it is, a work of art with a strong ethical lesson inherent throughout. The vulgar cackle of the critics echoed in Adele King's drawing-room, not to mention the Troubridges', and the aunts'! Constance must have had a thin time of it, for she too defended 'Dorian' as "weird, and wonderful and terrible in its imagery".

The family were just convalescing from Otho's divorce and flight— and now this! People would wonder! but people had always wondered about the Wildes—not that they did anything to discourage it. Yet Constance must have wondered uncomfortably what her husband had unleashed over his fine amber head. The furore raged through the heat of summer until smothered in the winter fogs which took 'Dorian's' creator to Paris to finish a play on a biblical theme called *Salome* and to seek financial backing for a play of a different kind, *Lady Windermere's Fan*.

This is where Constance's friends came in useful, and possibly Oscar had embarked on the scheme at her instigation. Part of the financial backing they hoped would come from Carlos Blacker, a cultivated man of private means, who possessed an extraordinary facility for learning languages, adding a new one to his repertoire every year. He and his wife Caroline moved in the same circle as the Ranee and Princess Alice. Both these ladies were in Paris and had met Oscar previously, when he was on honeymoon in Dieppe. The Princess, being a patron of theatre, was drumming up support for the *Fan* in the form of a house party where Carlos Blacker would meet Oscar.

At thirty-six, Oscar was in his prime and bore all the signs of a prosperous man, and with the good news from Paris it would appear that he was to be a successful man. Constance, who never doubted, despite views to the contrary, that he would become famous, allowed herself a little smile that all London was beginning to echo the epigrams and witticisms of the Apostle of Aestheticism. Beneath all the affectation there was always a great simplicity, implicit in the Irish race, and Constance, who was half Irish herself, wished there was more of the latter. For Oscar, with approaching fame, although still an affectionate husband and father, was growing away from the House Beautiful. Now, after eight years of marriage, she realized that there were times when he needed his home and times when he did not. He said once, "I pity with all my heart those poor creatures who have no home."

Meantime, the cigarette-rolling founder of Theosophy, Madam Blavatsky, had died, and to some extent her mantle fell onto the equally competent Annie Besant, whose occult lectures were well attended. Frank Miles, the one-time friend of Oscar, who had been committed to a lunatic asylum, had also died. And with these, one could fancifully say that the "aesthetic poses" of the Wildes had died too; they were embarking on what some have called Oscar's "second phase". Success was assured. The years of plenty were ahead; yet as far as Constance was concerned, they could well have been called the lean years.

8

Introducing Shadows

When *Lady Windermere's Fan* appeared on the London stage in February 1892, Oscar Wilde established his position as a successful writer on both sides of the English Channel. It was also the fateful year of his introduction to Lord Alfred Douglas, a younger son of the eighth Marquess of Queensberry. It was unfortunate for the Wildes that father and son hated each other. On Alfred's part the hatred grew out of his father's treatment of his mother, who had divorced the Marquess in 1887 on the grounds of cruelty and adultery.

Young Lord Alfred decided to ask the eminent playwright to get him out of some "appalling mess" at Oxford. Wilde did so and through this action lost the esteem of Sir George Lewis, the solicitor who had been instrumental in getting him launched on the American tour fifteen years before. This was to be the pattern of their friendship: Douglas gained something, Wilde losing eventually everything.

Lady Queensberry, Alfred's beautiful and indulgent mother, referred to him as 'Bosie', a pet name which was a shorter version of the infant 'Boysie'. It was she who warned Oscar of her son's two chief faults, one being vanity, the other "being all wrong about money". She could also have mentioned his "inherited fits of almost epileptic rage" and streaks of abject sullenness, but Oscar was to suffer these defects later. She did admit that she was afraid to take her younger son to task because, "he gets so angry when he's spoken to." Indeed, her letters to Wilde regarding the young man always ended with, "Pray do not let Alfred know that I have written to you."

Such was the nature of the latest disciple who accompanied the poet Lionel Johnson to tea in the book-lined study at Tite Street. Afterwards Oscar took him to Constance's sitting-room and introduced the 'Golden Boy' to her. This led to an invitation to the Queensberry ball, and later her ladyship asked the Wildes, children and all, to spend the summer on the Queensberry estate in Scotland. Douglas was to say this of Constance:

> I liked her and she liked me. She told me, about a year after I first met her, that she liked me better than any of Oscar's other friends. She frequently came to my mother's house and was present at a dance which my mother gave during the first year of my acquaintance with her husband. After the débâcle I never saw her again, and I do not doubt that Ross and others succeeded in poisoning her mind against me, but up to the very last hour of our acquaintance, we were the best of friends. Honesty compels me to say that Oscar during the time I knew him was not very kind to his wife. He certainly had been (as he often told me) very much in love with her, and the marriage was purely a love match. At the time I first met him he was still fond of her but became impatient and sometimes snubbed her, and he resented and showed that he resented, the attitude of slight disapproval she often adopted toward him.

As shall be seen later, Constance's attitude to Douglas was merely that of a gracious and hospitable hostess.

But, back in February, on a Saturday night, with a scintillating audience, *Lady Windermere's Fan* at the St James's Theatre was a huge success. Oscar had taken his mother's advice and was present. He had been temperamental with George Alexander, the producer, and had threatened to veto the opening night, but 'Speranza' had advised him against such foolishness. He had reserved a box not only for himself but for Constance, Lord Alfred Douglas and Mrs Ada Leverson, whom Oscar called 'the Sphinx'. She belonged to the cultivated and elegant Jewish society in London, contributed witty articles to *Punch* and satirized very cleverly anyone or anything that took her fancy. She was Wilde's closest woman friend—her wit providing a perfect foil for his, and all the disciples doted on her. At this first night, Constance was singled out by the Press as "looking charming in her pale brocaded Charles 1st styled gown with its long tabbed bodice, slashed sleeves and garnished with lace and pearls".

The huge and startling success of the *Fan* swept away all the unwholesomeness of 'Dorian Gray' and set the seal on Oscar's fame as a playwright. When the curtain came down for the last time, the audience leapt to its feet and roared for the author. Even the Prince of Wales joined in the calls with royal fervour and forgot his differences with Lillie Langtry, who sat in the box opposite. The curtain was held back, and there was Oscar, big, handsome, a lighted cigarette between his fingers, a smile parting his lips, his evening coat open and a green carnation nestling in his buttonhole. As Constance watched him talking to the audience, buttering them up, titillating their vanity, she may have thought of the 'flop' of *Vera* in America, and the censure which had surrounded 'Dorian Gray', and revelled all the more in this astounding triumph.

The year of the *Fan* was a marvellous year. The Wildes received more invitations to country houses than they could accept, and the boys were invited to more children's parties than were good for them. One fancy-dress party was causing some concern to Chelsea parents in general, and the Wildes in particular. Cyril and Vyvyan, now six and seven were adamant in their desire for sailor suits. But their father was having none of it. He could see neither imagination nor merit in navy-blue serge and thought that Cyril, with his curly hair, would make an admirable 'Bubbles' and Vyvyan in a velvet suit would make an admirable 'Little Lord Fauntleroy'. Although this view was received with howls of contempt, the orders were given for the clothes. The following week the Wildes were holding a reception in the drawing-room—perhaps to celebrate Constance's Uncle Charles Hemphill becoming Solicitor-General for Ireland—and the boys sent to get dressed in their outfits to give the guests a preview. They trotted off, mutiny in every step. At the sound of their return, every eye was set on the grand entrance. In came the boys, one after the other, not in their fancy dress clothes but entirely without. Absolutely naked! They deserved a standing ovation for sheer enterprise, and no doubt got it. The children had made their point. Sailor suits were ordered at once, from the best naval tailoring establishment.

At least one of Constance's contemporaries admits to her possessing a sense of humour, albeit a subtle one, and that was Louise Jopling. Louise was a professional artist, who noted gleefully that there was talk of limiting the number of women at the Royal Academy schools because they carried all the prizes away from the men! She lectured on such controversial subjects as "There is no sex in Art." While Constance was away, Oscar had been invited to a house party at Cranley Place, the home of the artist, noted for its pinewood rafters in the studio, antique tapestry and Millais frescos. As the guests posed for the usual formal photographs, Louise, according to Mr Montgomery Hyde, suggested they should get up a scene: "I'll make love to Oscar," she said, "and you must all be shocked!" When Constance called to see Louise at her art school in Clareville Grove and was shown the photograph of this Amazon of a woman with olive skin and brown hair, tall, broad and thrice married, with her arms about Oscar's neck in an affectionate pose, her only comment—on which one could put an intriguing interpretation—was "Poor Oscar!"

Another impression comes from William Rothenstein, the artist, who recalls in *Men and Memories* that,

> Constance Wilde was not clever but she had distinction and candour. With brown hair framing her face and a liberty hat, she looked like a drawing by William Crane. One of Constance Wilde's intimate friends was Mrs. Walter Palmer [her daughter Gladys later married the Ranee's middle son, Bertram] who was a close friend of the novelist George Meredith and his daughter, Mariette. One eventful evening George Meredith came to a party at Mrs. Palmer's—I went down to supper with Constance Wilde and when she discovered me to be a whole hearted Meredith fan she took me to meet great man.

Harry de Windt, the Ranee's brother, referred to Constance as being "A highly cultured woman, with a fine brain; but rarely made any public parade of her knowledge. Many who found her a most delightful and gracious hostess would have been surprised if they had realised what force and depth of character, what acute power of reasoning and analysis lay behind the placid and beautiful exterior."

In the August of 1892 the Wildes had been *en famille* at Grove Farm, Felbrigg, near Cromer in Norfolk, where Oscar was trying to get to grips with another play *A Woman of No Importance*. Between the ebb and flow of various guests, Oscar spent two or three hours a day on the golf links. Some previous biographers have said that Wilde did not know a driver from a putter, and invented the interest to get away from his wife. One would hope that a man of Wilde's imagination would be capable of a more convincing excuse! It is also said that Constance knew so little about her husband that she believed him!

Why should she not have believed him? There are many references which point to the golf interest; Robert Ross considered his friend an "enthusiastic if indifferent golfer". Sets of clubs were sold off an knock-down prices at the enforced Tite Street sale. Moreover, Lady Queensberry recalls Wilde playing golf while staying at her house. Whoever suggested Constance's gullibility was wrong. It was impossible for a woman of her comprehension to be so taken in.

After Felbrigg it was decided they should go and stay at Babbacombe Cliff, and Constance, leaving Oscar at the farm, went on ahead to have some time alone with her beloved 'Mia Madre'. As it happened, her ladyship was due to travel abroad for several months, which meant that Constance and her family were welcome to stay until her return. It must have given Constance immense pleasure to show them the delights and splendours of the temple of Pre-Raphaelite Art where she had spent the happiest days of her life. Those who have not the stomach for a fussy décor would regard it as a little overdone, for above the door of each bedroom was the name of a flower which depicted the style of the wallpaper inside—William Morris paper, of course. Hence the daffodil room, marigold room etc. The drawing-room walls were festooned with masterpieces by Rossetti and Burne-Jones and were referred to as Wonderland. Although Babbacombe Cliff was extremely arty, it was not a mausoleum but wore the air of a small country manor-house. Of the two children it was more likely to be Vyvyan, the gentler boy, who would appreciate the artistic qualities of the place. Cyril, on the other hand, was able to expend his boundless energy roaming the vast gardens, which in places resembled a small wood, and rambling down to a wide sandy bay—a much better proposition than the Chelsea Hospital Gardens, which was their playground when at home in Tite Street. The beach below the house could have been almost a private one in those days, and Oscar, who was a keen swimmer, took his sons sailing and fishing. As enthusiastic on the beach as in the nursery, he would remove his shoes and stockings, for casual dress then consisted of knee-breeches of the plus-fours kind, wade into pools in search of crabs, play hectic games with a huge coloured ball and do all the things a loving father dreams up at the seaside.

Oscar, naturally, adored the house. It was among the first to have a central heating system installed. It would have needed it, too, for the entrance hall and some of the floors on ground level were laid in marble and mosaics: very picturesque and cool in the heat of the summer months, but, come winter, they must have been frightfully cold. The fireplaces were small for the size of rooms, and the wind howling under the doors from across the bay would have made it exceedingly draughty—it is not to be wondered at that her ladyship wintered abroad.

The Pre-Raphaelite surroundings obviously suited Oscar's muse, for he wrote *A Woman of No Importance* while he was there. So, with her husband working happily and no distractions from doting disciples, why did Constance decide to break from domestic bliss—if such it was—and spend the rest of the vacation in Italy with the Ranee and the Carlos Blacker family? Had she hoped that in the long summer of '92 a measure of understanding between herself and Oscar would re-assert itself? The fact of their bedroom relationship never being restored must have irked so sexual a woman keenly. Were there arguments and scenes, or did she just fancy a change? Whatever the reason, no sooner had she left for the Continent than Alfred Douglas and his tutor arrived to enjoy what was, by all accounts, a highly hilarious time.

Despite Lord Alfred Douglas's protestations that Constance preferred him to any of the other disciples, she resented his interruptions of her husband's work; for, just as Robbie Ross had kept Oscar from working in the early days of their marriage, so this honey-haired youth, if not at Tite Street for luncheon or tea, would call to whisk Oscar away to drink, talk, smoke, meet people—anything but work.

Robbie Ross, too, was showing signs of resentment, and he became Constance's ally in fellow-feeling, for, among the coterie of aspiring young men who always hung about Oscar, he had been the favourite one. Now he too was being eased from the centre of the stage to join Constance in the wings and to watch young Douglas inch his way into that special place. That Robbie was jealous is understandable, for Bosie was a very attractive young man, fair, slimly built, possessed of a petulant boyishness which added to his charm. Moreover, he was a poet of no mean standing and was translating *Salome* into French for a performance in Paris. What made matters worse from Robbie's point of view was that Oscar was now famous, a celebrity, and it was Bosie, the newcomer, and not himself who was shaping Oscar's magnificence.

It has been levelled against Constance that she was not strong enough to hold Oscar steady against the tide of success which was beginning to sweep him off course. No one, not even his favourite

Adele Schuster or 'the Sphinx', nor a herd of wild horses, would have altered the course he believed the gods had mapped out for him to tread.

If Constance was a little apprehensive of success, she did not show it, for although Oscar was becoming extravagant beyond his means, he was still fond of her and was a loving and indulgent father. At times she could not help being concerned that people were talking about his outrageous views on life—not to mention death and the hereafter—but people had always talked about him, and he had never discouraged it. "To pass through life unnoticed," he said, "is the most ostentatious form of obscurity!" And at one time she had revelled in his reputation as an Aesthetic young man who was setting society at odds. In an introspective mood she may indeed have felt that he was going a little too far for their Victorian society. So far and so fast that she could not keep pace with him.

Back in London in the spring of 1893, *A Woman of No Importance* played to packed audiences at the Haymarket. Easter had been spent at the Burne-Joneses' large, rambling house in Kensington, and the entire house party took seats in the stalls. It was a stupendous success. The papers raved. "Mr. Wilde's dramatic work is on the highest plane of English drama . . . he has no rival among his fellow workers for the stage."

At such times, when her husband was fêted and idolized, when he had the world at his feet, Constance alternated between apprehension and intoxicating elation. Her husband had achieved the fame she had hoped for, and she was not certain how to cope with it. His friendships, like his life-style, were becoming more extravagant, and she would have to try to come to terms with them—for her own sake and that of the boys.

After the resounding success, life became a kaleidoscope of events, of journeys and junketings and the petty squabbles of domesticity. If it irked Constance to see the disciples wasting Oscar's time, it began to irk him also, for his mind was teeming with ideas for a new play, and he could not get on with it.

At this time Alfred Douglas, having failed to take his degree, asked Wilde to go up to Goring-on-Thames with him, as under the circumstances he did not want to go and stay at home. While at Goring Bosie saw a nice country property called 'The Cottage'; it was white walled, light and airy with attic rooms and large gardens. He liked the place at once and urged Oscar to rent it for three months or so, which, of course, he did—with a view to getting on with *An Ideal Husband*, for which he was under contract to John Hare. There was another request. Bosie wanted his own Oxford servant taken into service for the summer, and this too was arranged, all at Wilde's expense.

Apart from anything else, Oscar was glad to be away from London because of gossip regarding Willie. Although Oscar courted scandal, he was terrified of it. Perhaps that was why he courted it. However, when it concerned his family, he did not like it. No doubt it brought back memories of the scandal from which his father had never recovered. Willie, because he was the brother of the famous Oscar, was singled out for special treatment by the Press. Marriage with the rich American woman was not going at all well.

"No good to me by day or night! says Mrs. Willie Wilde," shrieked one headline.

"Tired of Willie!" shrieked another.

Such a public display annoyed Oscar and distressed Constance. But Lady Wilde took it all with what could have been a self-protective obtuseness, or innocence. "Willie won't get up and won't work," she wrote. "Mrs. Leslie has stopped all his allowance, so he has nothing now but what he earns!"

Soon the divorce hit the headlines, and Constance was in receipt of another letter from her mother-in-law:

What do you think [she wrote], as soon as Willie returned to London he re-married! Almost at once! She is Miss Florence Lees; but the marriage must be kept quiet until Florence can bring her step-mother to approve of it, for she has £2,000 to leave when she dies and has declared her intention of altering her will if her daughter marries Willie! Apart from that, Miss Lees has only £50 a year, and that, Willie assures me, just dresses her. They are both coming here in March and as they have no income I am alarmed at the prospect. I have an immense dislike to sharing my house with Miss Lees with whom I have nothing in common at all.

Poor 'Speranza', her hopes of "wonderful wives" for both her sons seemed in jeopardy as far as Willie was concerned. Constance felt for her and visualized the old woman living on her memories of past glory and brooding over the troubles of her eldest. But it was not long before Miss Lees—'Speranza' could not yet bring herself to call her 'Mrs Willie'—did appear, and her soft heart melted, and then her letters were full of 'Mrs Willie'.

'Mrs Oscar' does not appear to have stayed at the Cottage, which still exists under the name of the Ferry House it is grandly extended and owned by Sir Arthur T. Harris Bart. Oscar only came up to town for the royal marriage, which took place on 6th July, between the Duke of York and Princess May of Teck, at the Chapel Royal, St James's Palace.

The Goring experiment bore the hallmark of failure, an expensive one. Apart from not fulfilling his contract, it cost Wilde £1,500 in three months. Plain country fare was not sufficient for the Golden Boy's palate; hampers of gourmet food and wines had to be ordered from town. Bosie and he quarrelled several times, the latter leaving in a huff but always returning. Such temperamental goings-on were not conducive to writing comedies; neither were visitors, who, fancying a day or two in the country, came in droves.

One such young man, an aspiring poet, Theodore Wratislaw, left a memoir of a week-end at the Cottage. It shows Oscar in a happy light, in white flannels and pink shirt. No one else was staying that week-end, and we catch a rare glimpse of Cyril. Wratislaw writes, "Breakfast was illuminated not only by Wilde's pervasive smile but the unexpected appearance of a small boy . . . one of his two sons . . . he was possibly the most beautiful child I have ever seen, sturdy and strong with a mass of golden curls and large violet eyes. He had come down from town that morning to spend part of the day." And later, he continues,

"We proceeded to the banks of the Thames and a boathouse, and Oscar commenced to row myself and the child in a sculling boat . . . during lunch an amusing incident occurred. . . . It is possible I overlooked at the moment the Irish ancestry of Oscar and made some slighting remark about Home Rule. The small boy flushed with anger, and violently demanded whether I was not a Home Ruler? I was both astonished and amused and was trying to think of some reply suitable for the juvenile politician when Oscar interposed, throwing peace on troubled waters. 'Ah' said he, 'My own idea is that Ireland should rule England.' I was able to laugh without needing to find a reply, and so the thorny matter dropped."

The unfortunate Theodore, apart from wearing city clothes, caught a cold and retired early. On Monday, when he wanted to make up for lost time and to hear more of Oscar's talk, the latter went in from the garden and said he was going to work. "I proceeded to be very bored for a couple of hours. Toward one o'clock I strayed into the drawing room. Oscar was seated at a table with some large manuscript books before him and turned round with a smile at my entrance, I ventured to enquire how he was getting on. 'I can't get on at all,' he said with a renewed smile, 'I have not an idea in my head, I can do nothing!' "

And so, the Goring jaunt having ended, Oscar returned to London. There are signs at this time, and no wonder, of Constance becoming anxious about their household finances. Her husband through indolence had broken his contract with John Hare, who was now pressing for the completion of *An Ideal Husband*, and Wilde had not even started it! Being more than capable of managing her own financial affairs she was impatient with Oscar for his mindless extravagance. Fortunately, the two men quarrelled, with the result that Douglas kept away for a week and the first part of the play was completed. But the second week Douglas, wanting to resume the friendship, arrived at noon. He would stand there, indolently smoking, gently whisking his gold-topped cane, smiling and talking until 1.30, then persuade Oscar to take him to lunch at the Café Royal until 3.30. Bosie then disappeared to his club, only to re-appear at tea-time. They dined either at Tite Street or at the Savoy and did not separate until after midnight, supper at Williss bringing the day to a close.

Constance found herself resenting the young man even more. She was not merely jealous; such an emotion had been evident many times before, ever since the advent of Ross. The hold which Alfred exercised over her husband was far more disturbing. Nothing was too good for him, nothing was too much trouble; his welfare and what the young man was going to make of his life seemed Oscar's sole concerns. Constance was as powerless in the tide of events as she had ever been. Alfred Douglas was the first, in retrospect, who had the colossal nerve to blame Constance for not taking the initiative. Others have taken their cue from him, saying it was not good enough that she should have stood by and hoped for some exorcism, for the removal of Bosie. But she had the perception to see that it would only have made her own position more wearisome—that of the aggrieved wife.

At last there came the longed-for break. After another spate of revolting quarrels between Wilde and Douglas, Lady Queensberry sent her son off to Egypt, and there he stayed for three months. Oscar refused point blank to correspond with him. The last three acts of *An Ideal Husband* were finished, and two other plays of a different nature, *A Florentine Tragedy* and *La Sainte Courtesane*.

Oscar's refusal to answer his young friend's letters resulted in a flurry of telegrams and a suicide threat to ginger things up a little. It worked. Oscar, with his wife's support, dashed off to Paris to stay the lad's hand, with the result that Bosie was re-instated to his former glory.

Constance must have been uneasy that the mad social whirl with Bosie was on again, and yet why did she put a word in for him? Perhaps the suicide threat and the apprehension of being involved in a scandal was at the back of her mind; Queensberry, they both knew, would make capital out of such a tragedy. Another supposition could be that, in the intervening several months which Oscar reckoned it would take before he could bring himself to communicate with Douglas, his wife hoped that the fascination would dissipate into so much hot air.

It was not to be. Did she really think or expect that anything would have changed? Bosie's aristocratic figure came swaggering into their lives again, dispensing turmoil and trouble with a charming largesse. 'A devil of a fellow', a beautiful and disobedient angel who had fallen from grace.

Soon another element was introduced into the Oscar/Bosie whirl, another twist to cause Constance further unease. The Marquess of Queensberry and his son, Lord Alfred, began to vent their hatred of each other not merely in cards, letters and telegrams but in public places. The 'Mad Marquess' openly objected to Oscar's relationship with his son; yet, instead of cutting the friendship or at least playing it cool, both men went out of their way to antagonize the enraged nobleman by flaunting it.

It was daunting for a woman of Constance's sensitivity to stand by and watch her husband becoming the bone of contention, the pawn, between father and son, to watch him throw discretion to the winds— not that he was ever at all discreet. And yet Ada Leverson, whom Constance sometimes met at the Albemarle Club, did not appear anxious or worried. But then, Ada was not in her position; rumour and gossip did not affect her; neither had she two sons to think of and a battalion of relatives to placate.

Lady Wilde did not seem to have any misgivings either. She remarked on Oscar's "starring it in Paris—and that sleeves and trousers are so tight that you are remarked upon in the Boulevards." Unlike 'Speranza', Constance could not "rise above the miasma of the commonplace", although the rumours affecting Oscar could hardly be called "commonplace". What price unconventionality now? What had began as a delectable feast now resulted in gross over-indulgence, and at this stage she must have longed for the bread and cheese of normality. But as Mrs Oscar Wilde she was stuck with it, and wherever she went, with or without him, she would be conscious of what people were thinking.

But there was more to worry about, for the florid-faced Marquess, who had a reputation for, among other things, writing loathesome letters, hurled this missile at his son:

> Your intimacy with this man Wilde must either cease or I will disown you and stop all money and supplies. I am not going to try and analyse intimacy, and I make no charge, but to my mind to pose as a thing is as bad as to be it . . . no wonder people are talking as they are. Also, I hear on good authority, but this may be false, that his wife is petitioning to divorce him for sodomy and other crimes. Is this true or do you not know of it? If I thought the actual thing was true, and it became public property, I should be justified in shooting him on sight.

His son replied in a telegram: "What a funny little man you are." This put Queensberry in a mad frenzy of rushing about hotels and restaurants to warn managers that he would thrash the pair if he discovered them together on the premises. He followed this up later with a visit to Tite Street, more or less to repeat the letter and to add further threats. Oscar described the scene in his library: the Marquess "waving his small hands in the air in epileptic fury, his bully, or friend, standing between us he began to utter every foul word his foul mind could think of, and screamed the loathesome threats he afterwards carried out with such cunning". Oscar drove both him and his bully out and threatened to shoot him if he ever appeared at Tite Street again.

Whether Constance was at home when he called—and if she was, she must have heard something of the row—or if she had scented the rumours going about town, is not known. But she did notice the increasing flow of notes from Lady Queensberry to Oscar which were marked 'Private' and used to laugh and say they must be collaborating on a society novel. It was not until Oscar was in prison that he told his wife the real reason for the notes from Lady Queensberry. Although making light of the matter, Constance must have suspected the nature of the notes and had not brought her suspicions out in the open—probably recognizing that their relationship was already too finely balanced on a knife-edge to bear yet another discussion on Bosie and his role in their lives; or, perhaps the subject had become a kind of no-go area. However, Constance was aware of the nature of the letters because Lady Queensberry, getting nowhere with Oscar (who reckoned he had had enough of Bosie's mother trying to shift her responsibilities onto him who already had enough of his own), decided to treat Constance to a little note marked 'Private'. It was terse and to the point. Her ladyship was anxious and desperate with concern about her son's association with Oscar, which was fast becoming the talk of the town. Some of their acquaintances were cutting him and certain restaurants refusing him admission. Alfred had become the subject of the raised eyebrow and scurrilous gossip. Would Mrs Wilde, therefore, speak with her husband with a view to him never seeing her son again?

Whatever Constance's first reaction was, her second was that of indignation. How dare Lady Queensberry assume that it was Oscar who kept the friendship going, especially after the Egyptian affair? There was also the time when her husband had determined to see Sir George Lewis and request him to write to the Marquess saying that under no circumstnces would he ever allow Alfred "to enter my house, sit at my board, to talk to me, walk with me, or at any time be my companion at all". But then fate took a hand. The following morning the papers told of Bosie's eldest brother, Lord Drumlanrig, being found dead in a ditch, his gun discharged at the side of him. A verdict of accidental death was returned at the coroner's inquest. Under the circumstances, Oscar relented, and Bosie was once again returned to the fold.

H. Montgomery Hyde, in his book *Oscar Wilde*, relates how the eleventh Marquess of Queensberry told Mr Hyde that he was positive that his uncle Drumlanrig had taken his own life in the shadow of a suppressed scandal. He was rumoured to have been implicated in a homosexual affair with Lord Roseberry, and if Drumlanrig's father knew or thought that his eldest son had committed suicide under those circumstances, both his violent reaction and the mother's concern as to their younger son's relationship with Wilde have greater grounds than were previously suspected.

After Constance's indignation had settled, the peculiar cruelty of the words would strike home. "Would Mrs Wilde speak with her husband?" Could she? What good would it do now? Only to end in a scene rivalling those he had with Bosie, which would drive the wedge between them even deeper. That there was a wedge is evident. Oscar was less and less at Tite Street and was not even aware that Constance

Constance Wilde, poised,
competent and confident;
advocate of Women's
Suffrage and member of
the Women's Liberal
Federation

. and in her later years

Oscar Wilde at the
height of his succes
1894. This was the
photograph taken c
Wilde before his tri

Lord Alfred Bruce
Douglas, third son
the eighth Marque
Queensberry, whos
friendship brought
ruin and disgrace t
Wilde

HERE WAS ONCE

GRANDMA'S STORIES.

By Mrs. Oscar Wilde

With Colour Pictures by JOHN LAWSON.

E. P. DUTTON & COMPANY
31 West Twenty-Third Street
NEW-YORK.

ERNEST NISTER
24 St. Bride Street
LONDON E.C.

Printed at Nuremberg.

Title-page of Constance Wilde's book of children's stories inspired by
her maternal grandmother, and published in 1889

Constance Wilde at a ba[zaar]: a
contemporary pen and i[nk]
drawing

No. 16 Tite Street, Chel[sea,]
Constance Wilde's home [from]
1885 to 1895. The décor [was]
considered 'bizarre and
vaguely sinful'. The hous[e]
was re-numbered in 1931 [as]
No. 34

Her Serene Highness Princess Alice of Monaco; blonde, intelligent,
patron of the arts, and friend of Constance Wilde

Statue erected on the promenade at Babbacombe in 1901, of Lady
Mount Temple, a rich and remarkable patron of Pre-Raphaelite Art and
Constance Wilde's 'Mia Madre'

Lady Brooke, Ranee of Sarawak; a fascinating woman, gifted, eccentric and brave, and in whose company Constance spent the latter years of her life

St James's Church, Paddington, where Constance Lloyd married Oscar Wilde in 1884, and where her beloved Grandpapa Lloyd was buried six weeks later

had engaged a new Swiss governess over the past year to tutor the boys, who were due to go to school in the autumn.

Perhaps she envisaged the scene. Herself standing before him, strong in her simple grasp of a complex situation, strong with a simplicity which seemed in these latter days to have a stultifying effect on his imagination, his fun, his boyish, eager attitude to life. That disregard for the world she had so admired and which had made him the most fascinating member of a fascinating family, now mocked her resolve and, with its vast and as yet unclarified complications, frightened her. She felt herself to be small and mean and carping, playing the injured wife and causing Oscar to despise such commonplace emotions. Her protective instincts, not merely for Oscar but for their survival as a family, surfaced above self-pity and made her do something positive. She gathered together her favourite epigrams, poems and extracts from her husband's writings and publishing them under the title of *Oscariana*, letting it be known that Mrs Oscar Wilde had collated the edition. This literary endeavour was a show of solidarity to offset public opinion, for she dreaded to see her husband's name, like that of his father, involved in a scandal, even more than Lady Queensberry feared for her son.

While spending many hours alone studying the work of this highly sensitive and unconventional man who was her husband, she found herself reading his work as for the first time, with an objectivity not possible before. As though by divine revelation her eyes were opened; she understood and could see with a crystal clarity what there was about *The Portrait of Dorian Gray* which had so shocked Victorian susceptibilities. There was a kind of innocence about his early writings, an innocence which she recognized, and she mourned its passing. Some of his poems and certain phrases bore a strangely prophetic note about them which would hardly have cheered her up. And if anything, the study would make her profoundly aware of the changes that had taken and were taking place in the structure of both Oscar's world and her own. It was not that her image of Oscar had altered in any way, but it seemed he could no longer properly reflect himself. If he was being carried away on a tide, he could no longer resist, and he was dragging her with him. There could be no turning back; the tide was sweeping them all remorselessly on, and all she could hope for was to keep her head above the water, to survive and not be submerged, for the sake of Cyril and Vyvyan.

The man who was to bring out the publication of *Oscariana* was her friend Arthur Humphries, the manager of Hatchard's bookshop in Piccadilly, whom she met at Pre-Raphaelite Society meetings. She was also in the habit of calling in at the shop to indulge in friendly arguments of a philanthropic nature. There was a delightful archness in their relationship, and they kept in touch with each other until she died. There were two editions of the book, one in January and another to follow in the spring.

As for Oscar, he was hard-up and overdrawn at the bank. The quarter's rent for Tite Street was due, and the boys' school fees had to be paid. Contrary to some comments Oscar never lived off his wife's money. Her allowance was in the region of £800 a year—no wonder she was annoyed when Oscar worked his way through £1,500 in three months at Goring! Out of the £800 she would, at this stage, have to buy her own clothes, and there were the usual expenses of clubs, subscriptions, fares and hobbies—books being foremost. Although she was not a big spender like her husband, Constance's tastes could not by any means be classed as frugal. It is unlikely that Oscar ever approached her on the subject of money, for he used to despise his brother, Willie, for sponging off their mother. However, he always managed to raise a bit of cash off someone, and this time he borrowed from George Alexander, manager of the St James's Theatre, with which he paid his bills and had enough left to whisk Bosie Douglas off to Dieppe for three days. As for schools, it had been decided to send Cyril to Bedales, which had been opened the previous year as a 'pioneer school' by Mr J. H. Badley, while Vyvyan, being of a gentler nature, was to attend Hindlesham. The Wildes were considerate parents to take the different natures of their sons into account; most would have lumped both boys off to the same school just because they were brothers.

In the summer of 1894, when the storm clouds were beginning to gather, Constance, who, it seems, was going her own way and doing her own thing, took a seaside house on the Esplanade at Worthing for the children's summer holidays. It was probably all she could afford. And it was certain her husband could not afford anything. His creditors were pressing him, and Queensberry was chasing him. He was destitute and feeling very sorry for himself. Desperate and unhappy, there was no other option open to him than to swallow his pride and call at the Esplanade in Worthing, at the house which Constance had rented, to see if she would have him, and of course she did. He was hoping to settle down and start work on *The Importance of*

Being Earnest. But, like a fretful child, he grumbled about the confining nature of the house and complained that he had no room of his own in which to write. He had not much choice; it was a case of squeezing in with his family—or going to London, with his creditors and Queensberry in hot pursuit. He was so wrapped up in young Douglas that he considered the house not smart enough for his boyish soul and wrote urging him not to come.

Constance was not altogether happy and was certainly not free from strain, for the boys were fractious; lacking the extra room, she and Oscar were forced to dine with the governess and children, she knowing all the time how much he hated it. He was bored. It was all too natural for him. She regretted with a pained and searing regret that she could not join in his fanciful world of make-believe. He liked being surrounded by people of intense and colourful imagination, like Ada Leverson, who could talk his language, and thus an ordinary luncheon would have been "feasting on pomegranates", and a sea-front holiday house would have become girded with enchantment.

Occasionally the dimness of the dining-room was brightened by a visit from one of Oscar's disciples. And after a few days, what Constance must have dreaded most happened.

'The Golden Boy' put in an appearance.

9

Scandal

The effect of Alfred's presence could not have escaped her. Like the Prince Charming he was, he touched them all with his magic. Oscar was alive and vital again; the children were no longer fractious. There was laughter, games on the beach, fishing, bathing. Constance would sit beneath her parasol and watch gigantic castles or forts of sand loom up where Cyril could hide and pelt the unsuspecting with sand or seaweed.

If the possibility had not occurred to Constance before that her husband's 'pose', as the Marquess put it, was not a 'pose' at all, it was here at Worthing that the truth became painfully obvious. Oscar was so besotted, so carried away, so impervious, that restraint had gone to the winds. When Bosie was in a good mood, Oscar had eyes for no one else, and Constance, not having seen them together at such close quarters for some time, would have been catapulted into revelation. It did not need much: a look from beneath Oscar's heavy-lidded eyes, a touch, little attentions which had once been hers, were now his. At first she would take refuge in unbelief. Self-protection would suggest hero-worship on Bosie's part, and with Oscar the old story of an older man's admiration for his lost youth. Then reality would take over with such questions as, 'How long had it been going on?' A procession of disciples passed before her bewildered eyes, beginning with Robbie Ross. A hundred little pieces must have clicked into place. How many people, she was bound to wonder, knew or guessed? And how much longer could the dreadful truth be kept from 'the Mad Marquess'? Another knife twisted her emotions. No wonder their marital relations had never been re-established; Oscar had found another outlet for his passion, with young men. To have lost him to another woman would have been devastating, but to be rejected for a man was unbelievable and utterly humiliating. Lady Wilde, regarding Sir William's infidelities, could say with theatrical grandeur, "I am above the miasmas of the commonplace." But this relationship was no commonplace adultery. It was a criminal offence, a hideous crime about which headlines screamed from the papers . . . police raided premises . . . there were fights . . . and prison. When the revelation came, Constance was saddled with it. She could not, dare not confide in, or discuss it with, anyone who remotely understood. In the eyes of the law, to form a relationship with a person of the same sex was neither natural, malady nor weakness, but criminal. She was to wonder how far it had gone. Kisses? Caresses? Henry Somerset had been found in the arms of his footman. She would recall details from the newspapers, details both salacious and sordid; and all that was involved in the unnatural and nameless would no longer have happened to someone else—it was no longer their scandal but could soon be hers.

Reticence in those days being what it was, and the all-time low of the relationship between Oscar and his wife being what it was, there is no evidence of her at that stage having tackled the two, or even Oscar, about the situation. Putting the scene in context, and the criminal aspect of it, it would be a little like accusing him of murder. If she remained silent, she would at least have a little of her marriage left. If she confronted her husband with what she knew, it could drive him, in the state he was now in, to Alfred Douglas altogether. Whether her silence or manner conveyed her knowledge to the pair is open to conjecture, but Bosie's stay was short. He left for London. Then, when Constance too decided to give up the house and return home, Bosie returned and persuaded Oscar to take him for a few days' luxury at the Metropole Hotel in Brighton.

So, while her husband was piling up more credit with his lover in Brighton and struggling to finish *The Importance of Being Earnest* at the same time, Constance was back in Tite Street struggling with reality.

The House Beautiful echoed to shouts of the carefree boys engaged in a last frenzy of activity before being packed off to their respective schools. Constance supervised the sewing of name-tapes onto new clothes, for at ten years old Cyril was growing fast, and she checked the dispatch of their travelling trunks and replenishment of tuck-boxes. There were good-bye visits, when Cyril and Vyvyan, stiffly dressed and immaculate, were taken to their relatives to pay their respects and receive additions to their term's pocket money.

When the boys had gone and the governess had been dismissed, and with Oscar away for days on end with Bosie Douglas, Constance had plenty of time to wallow in dreadful indecision. Even the relatives were noticing Oscar's absences, and Oscar knew they noticed, for on passing Adrian Hope in the street, he remarked, "I know what you are thinking, 'There goes that dreadful Mr. Wilde leaving Constance alone again!' "

As if to drive home the danger of scandal, the autumn brought to the public's avid interest the sensational news of yet another police raid. This time it was a club in Fitzroy Street where eighteen men were arrested, two of them dressed "in female attire". Speculation and rumour concerning Wilde flared up again. The latest being that, if Wilde had not two plays running in the West End and was not on speaking terms with the Prince of Wales, he too would be 'inside' for his conduct, like the Fitzroy Street boys.

If Constance considered flight, it was dismissed. There must be no straws for the "screaming, mad Marquess" to clutch at, for her flight would seem like a corroboration of his suspicions. There was, of course, divorce, and as rumour already had it, she had grounds for such. But divorce was a messy business, as she well knew from Otho's experience and Willie Wilde's. The scandal, the disgrace of it, the consequent shunning of society for innocent and guilty alike: the guilty for having sinned, the innocent for having found out that they had sinned. Otho had gone to Switzerland to avoid the public gaze which had tormented his scholarly soul. Lord Henry Somerset's wife had petitioned for divorce and was refused admittance to the best drawing-rooms. It was as though Society punished her for making a fuss. Constance's upbringing had been a confirmation of this creed, that reality must be ignored. Her contempt for this creed, fostered by the influence of the Pre-Raphaelites and the Aesthetic code, had, during the past few years of Oscar's success, been gently eroded, so that by now what the newspapers called a 'hush-up' was very desirable. She may well have reflected bitterly that only people with strong minds and hearty outlooks—only the brave people like John Ruskin, Lady Archie Campbell, Otho's first wife, Nellie, Annie Besant and Lady Wilde—could survive the ravages of sensational scandal. Her protective instinct, already fostered by the championing of her father and grandfather, combined with the loyalty which her brother had recognized years earlier as being her chief characteristic, soon took over and emerged from any invective. It would not be through her that Vyvyan and Cyril would see their father's name on the hoardings, as Oscar had seen the name of his father. She shed many tears of frustrated bewilderment that Oscar, who loved his children so much, should blatantly jeopardize not only his own brilliant future but the future of two innocent children who worshipped him.

Another emotion in the merry-go-round of whirling reactions was that of jealousy. She had always resented the disciples taking him away from writing and home, but this friendship with Bosie had been different from the beginning—all the quarrelling and making-up to which she had been privy, even to urging him at least to write while Bosie was in Egypt. How she must have wished otherwise, for her husband, despite his vagaries and the success going to his head, had somehow over the years maintained a particular rapport with her, a bond which was always there. And, whatever happened, she had believed that, because of it, they would always remain together as a family. Resentment too would play its part, and as her feelings of desolation grew, resentments would pile up, one on top of the other, to make a monstrous mountain of it. While she had been paying the tradespeople out of her own allowance, Oscar had been lavishing presents he could not afford on Alfred, and others—that much, that there were others, she now admitted. There was also resentment because of the years she had slept alone, while he had been taking his fill elsewhere in so monstrous a manner; resentment too that people would be regarding her either as ineffectual or, what was worse, in a dreadful kind of *ménage à trois*. There was no relief, for, lastly, she would feel herself deprived above all else, because of the very nature of her anxiety, of the most elementary consolation, that of having someone to confide in, to talk it over with, to advise her. Mrs Wilde was indeed the unhappiest woman in London.

The publication, anonymous at first, of a book by Robert Hichens, called *The Green Carnation*, did nothing to help Constance. The central characters were unmistakably Oscar, as 'Esmé Amarinth', and

Alfred Douglas as 'Reggie Hastings'. The book was an acid skit on their extravagant relationship and aspects of aesthetic thought. We may be sure that Constance read it as analytically as she had read for *Oscariana*. Passages such as the following by Esmé Amarinth deepened her apprehension considerably:

> How I hate the word 'natural', to me it seems all that is middle class, all that is the essence of jingoism, all that is colourless . . . certain things are classed as unnatural—for all the people born in to the world. Individualism is not allowed to enter into the matter. A child is unnatural if it hates its mother. A mother is unnatural if she does not wish to have children. A man is unnatural if he never falls in love with a woman. A boy is unnatural if he prefers looking at pictures to playing cricket, or dreaming over the white, naked beauty of a Greek statue to a game of football under Rugby rules. If our virtues are not cut on a pattern, they are unnatural. If our vices are not according to rule, they are unnatural. We must be good naturally, we must sin naturally, we must live naturally and die naturally. . . . There are only a few people in the world who dare defy this grotesque code of rules that have been drawn up by that fashionable mother, Nature, and they defy in secret with the door locked and the key in their pockets; always in trepidation of the footsteps of the detective in the street outside.

"Detectives in the street outside." The phrase would conjure up all the lurid Press reports of police raids and flights and arrests, and hitherto unheard-of words such as 'pimps' and 'renters' and 'male brothels'! There had been an affair of the same kind at Dublin Castle; that too was well publicized.

Mrs Wilde was well aware of the danger, albeit she was as helpless in the hands of fate as her husband was in the toils of young Douglas. If she remonstrated or pleaded with Oscar about giving up the scandalous relationship with Douglas because of malicious gossip, he had the perfect answer. He was not giving in to Queensberry and his ilk. The old man would make capital out of it, bruiting it all over town that he had brought Oscar Wilde to heel. He was not giving in to a bully's threats. To go back was impossible. He had to go on. Knowing him, she was well aware of the streak which made him dice with disaster, the urge which drove him on and on, pushing and poking at society, seeing how far he could go in shocking them. If she could not, like her mother-in-law, "rise above the miasmas of the commonplace", then she must, like her relatives, like Grandmama Atkinson, like her mother, pretend normality, put on a good face—perhaps she even thought of putting on a bustle, but she did not.

In November 1894 an article in *To-day* entitled 'Mrs. Oscar Wilde at Home' gives further insight into her character.

Like her husband, poet, playwright and wit, Mrs. Oscar Wilde may be truly called an apostle of the beautiful. She has in a quiet and unobtrusive manner made everything that concerns the beautifying of the home a special study, and her exquisite embroidery and needlework is appreciated by a large circle of friends and acquaintants, although she has never yet been persuaded to exhibit anything in one of the many yearly "shows" which make a speciality of the blending of the arts and crafts.

Mr. and Mrs. Wilde have set up their household gods in one of the prettiest corners of old Chelsea, within a stone's-throw of the Walk once paced by the Sage of Chelsea and Jeannie Welsh Carlyle, by Dante Gabriel Rossetti, and George Eliot.

There is an utter lack of so-called aesthetic colouring in the house of which Mrs. Oscar Wilde is mistress; the scheme consisting as it does, of faded and delicate brocades, against a background of white or cream painting, is French rather than English.

Rare engravings and etchings form a deep frieze along two sides of the drawing-room, and stand out on a dull gold background, and the only touches of bright colour in the apartment are lent by two splendid Japanese feathers let into the ceiling, while, above the white, carved mantelpiece, a gilt-copper bas-relief, by Donaghue, makes living Mr. Oscar Wilde's fine verses, 'Requiescat.'

To most of Mrs. Oscar Wilde's visitors not the least interesting work of art in this characteristic sitting-room is a quaint harmony in greys and browns, purporting to be a portrait of the master of the house as a youth; this painting was a wedding present from Mr. Harper Pennington, the American artist, and is much prized by the wife of the original.

Even apart from this picture, Mrs. Wilde can boast of an exceptionally choice gallery of contemporary art. Close to a number of studies of Venice, presented by Mr. Whistler himself, hangs an exquisite pen-and-ink illustration by Walter Crane. An etching of Bastien Le Page's portrait of Sarah Bernhardt contains in the margin in a few kindly words written in English by the great tragedienne.

"I scarcely think myself competent to say much on decoration," observed my hostess, modestly. "Of course, those matters are so much questions of sentiment and feeling. I am, personally, often struck by the amount of over-decoration that is now the rule, rather than the exception in many houses."

"Then you think that the amateur decorator should always aim at simplicity?"

"Certainly," she replied, thoughtfully; "no one who has not tried them knows the value of uniform tints and a quiet scheme of colouring. One of the most effective effects in house decoration can be obtained by leaving, say, the sitting-room, pure cream or white, with, perhaps, a dado of six or seven feet from the ground. In an apartment of this kind, ample colouring and variety will be introduced by the furniture, engravings, and carpet; in fact, but for the trouble of keeping white walls in London clean, I do not think there can be anything prettier and more practical than this mode of decoration, for it is both uncommon and easy to carry out. I am not one of those," continued Mrs. Wilde, "who believe that beauty can only be achieved at considerable cost. A cottage parlour may be, and often is, more beautiful, with its unconsciously achieved harmonies and soft colouring, than a great reception-room, arranged more with a view to producing a magnificent effect. But, I repeat, of late, people, in their wish to decorate their homes, have blended various periods, colourings and designs, each perhaps beautiful in itself, but producing an unfortunate effect when placed in juxtaposition. I object also to historic schemes of decoration, which nearly always make one think of the upholsterer, and not of the owner of the house."

"I believe that flowers are now playing a very great part in decoration?"

"Yes, but it is possible to have too many flowers in a room, and I think that scattering cut blossoms on a table-cloth is both a foolish and a cruel custom, for long before dinner is over the poor things begin to look painfully parched and thirsty for want of water. A few delicate flowers in plain glass vases produce a prettier effect than a great number of nosegays, and yet, even though people may see that something is wrong many do not realise how easily a charming effect might be produced with the same materials, somewhat differently disposed."

"And what do you think of the present craze for Japanese art?"

Mrs. Wilde smiled.

"I wonder how many people know that the greater number of cheap Japanese fans and screens, to say nothing of trays, etc., sold in this country, are specially made for the English market. That this is so, is easily proved to anyone who knows anything of Japanese life. The Japs have a horror of a black background, and all their work is done in light, pale colourings. Again, a Japanese native room is furnished with dainty simplicity, and one flower and one pot supply the Jap's aesthetic longing for decoration. When he gets tired of his flower and his pot, he puts them away, and seeks for some other scheme of colour produced by equally simple means. As for fans, they are, of course, in Japan made for use and not for show. I think that even if people would only try to see that the articles they have in daily use are beautiful, and devoted a little less time to simply buying useless nick-nacks, whose only raison d'être is their supposed artistic worth, the problem of many a would-be House Beautiful would be solved."

"I believe, Mrs. Wilde, that you do a good deal of embroidery."

"Yes, but I do not claim to have any special ideas on the subject, I am, just now, anxious to learn Chinese needlework, such very beautiful effects seem to be produced by its means."

"And do you think that such an exhibition as the Arts and Crafts is of much use from a practical point of view?"

"The Arts and Crafts Exhibitions seem to serve two purposes. They produce emulation amongst the workers, and awaken curiosity and latent artistic instincts among the general public, and I should imagine that the exhibitions are of unmixed good, if sufficient time is allowed for the production of new and original work. I speak as an entire outsider, one to whom all decorative work, whatever form it may take, is intensely interesting, and who consequently thoroughly enjoys these exhibitions."

An interesting glimpse into Mrs. Oscar Wilde's tastes and surroundings is afforded by a glance through her autograph-book, a plain little volume cased in a charming book-cover made by herself. From the dedicatory verses on the first page, written by the author of "Salome" to his wife:

> 'I can write no stately proem,
> as a prelude to my lay;
> From a poet to a poem,
> I would 'dare' to say . . .'

to the last of the many characteristic utterances contained therein, every signature gives food for thought, and, oftener than not, reveals something of the writer.

"Our greatest happiness should be found in the happiness of others," declares Mr. G. F. Watts, the great painter, whose work has brought joy to so many. Sir Edwin Arnold drops into poetry with some pretty lines. George Meredith writes his little poem, "Love is winged for two." Sturdy independence is equally shown in the round, frank calligraphy of Robert Browning, and the more delicate American handwriting of Mark Twain; and under some ardently patriotic forecasts signed T. P. O'Connor. Mr. Arthur James Balfour dryly remarks, "Of all exercise of the human intelligence political prophecy is the most vain." Mr. Swinburne must have had his hostess's two boys in his mind when he transcribed in their mother's book his beautiful lines on childhood, and Mr. Walter Crane is represented by—

> "From your book I take a leaf,
> by your leave to leave and take;
> Art is long if life be brief,
> Yet on this page my mark I'll make."

And then comes John Bright's favourite quotation, "In peace sons bury their fathers. In war fathers bury their sons." Mr. Whistler contributes his long-suffering "Butterfly broken on the wheel," and the simple signature of Oliver Wendell Holmes, Sergeant, the American painter, John Ruskin, Henry Irving, Miss Ellen Terry, and many other familiar and unfamiliar names, evoke a vision of what should be a unique gathering of notable men and women.

Although Oscar spent most of his time staying at various hotels, he endeavoured to be home when his sons were on vacation from school and certainly put in an appearance in the Christmas holiday of '94, for Robert Sherard recalls dining with Wilde and his family on Christmas Day.

On 3rd January 1895 *An Ideal Husband* was the outstanding success the public had come to expect from so brilliant a dramatist. The Press were enthusiastic, and the Prince of Wales was congratulatory. The only blot on the landscape was the Marquess stepping up his campaign against Oscar's friendship with his son.

To antagonize the old man even further, Oscar blatantly and openly went to Algiers for two weeks with Bosie. They returned for *The Importance of Being Earnest*, the first night of which Constance did not attend, perhaps because she had heard rumours that the Marquess was out to make a disturbance at the theatre, but the police, being forewarned, refused his admittance, whereupon the Marquess, with puce face and bulging eyes, swore for all to hear that he would hunt Oscar Wilde down.

Constance regularly visited her mother-in-law to pass on the *Ladies' Pictorial* and to enjoy a "good old gossip". Oakley Street was silent now. No longer did the solid, dignified citizens need to part the curtains of their solid, ivy-clad houses at the clatter of hansom cabs bearing the literati to Speranza's salon. Neither did the Americans come from the Atlantic steamers moored at Chelsea Bridge. Those days of theatrical splendour had gone. Did Constance reflect upon the Wildes: Sir William, Willie and now Oscar? Indeed, the House of Wilde seemed fated—and the most horrific fate was in store for the most fascinating member of that fascinating family.

In the candle-lit drawing-room, Lady Wilde lifted her veil to tell Constance across the teacups, "Mrs Willie is expecting." The old lady, thrilled with the news, did not see disaster looming ahead for her younger son—or, with her singular obtuseness, did not want to. She was ecstatic over his success and raved that he had two successful plays in the West End, and that for *Earnest* all the men wore lily-of-the-valley in their buttonholes. Another subject of conversation was

Uncle Charles Hemphill, the Wildes' one-time near neighbour, who had been elected Liberal member for North Tyrone in the recent elections, and dearer to both their hearts, there was Cyril's half-term holiday, which was to be spent at home.

What Constance had not told her mother-in-law was that, since returning from Algiers, Oscar was living openly and at great expense at the Avondale Hotel with Alfred Douglas. This intelligence had been received in a note from Oscar delivered to Tite Street, a note which, in view of the Marquess's last words, must have filled her with instant foreboding. At one time she had not minded his frequent absences because he had been based at her home and not that of another woman. Now, he was based at a hotel—with a male lover.

The House Beautiful echoed with his absence, from the top of the dove-grey and yellow stairs to Oscar's bedroom and smoking-den. Ghosts would be everywhere. Ghosts of herself and Oscar when they were younger . . . ghosts in the nursery when Cyril was ill with measles and Oscar had been due out of town at Cambridge to dine with Robbie Ross . . . ghosts of the disciples wandered in and out of Tite Street . . . fair, dark, beautiful, intelligent, clever. All that was left now was for her to sit it out and to wait, like a victim, for the axe to fall.

The first blow came in the form of a letter from the Avondale Hotel. It had been delivered by hand. The second blow was that Cyril was not coming home for half term. The third filled her with foreboding. Oscar was coming to see her. It was important. Her disappointment at not having her son home and her reflection on how the boy would take it, were drowned in a sea of dreadful speculation. Tormented by a terrible sense of urgency, Constance knew it was all up. Just how events had come to a head, she was not to know until he told her. He was calling at nine o'clock; she must have counted the minutes and yet dreaded the passing of each one. Ears would be strained for the sound of a cab outside . . . for Arthur, their manservant, to open the door . . . murmured words in the hall, and there he would be, almost filling the doorway, huge in his fur coat against the February night.

Wilde had written to Robbie Ross asking him to come to the Avondale at 11.30 that night. So no doubt Constance would be the first to see or hear about the card which Queensberry had left at the Albemarle Club. If Oscar intended to sue Queensberry for libel, it was right that she should be told. The card bore the words, "To Oscar Wilde posing as a somdomite." The incorrect spelling was put down to the Marquess's apoplexy. Her natural response would be a breath-less appeal to ignore the card. No one but Oscar knew what was written on it; and a libel action must have been what she feared most. He too feared scandal, and yet the bizarre element to cast himself down and see what the gods cast up eventually won. What would Society think if he did not challenge Queensberry? Who, after all, had baited Oscar often enough. What was more, he was convinced that the Marquess had no evidence against him. By eleven o'clock he had gone back to await Robbie Ross at the Avondale, leaving Constance to the ghosts, to the spectre of dreaded scandal.

The libel action commanded the full attention of the Press. The thing Constance had feared came to pass. Scandal. To see his name, hers, on the front page, for all the world to see. There was even a paragraph about her and the boys. The Press had done its work in circulating the sensational news so well that the Wildes' position in Society was in jeopardy already, to the extent that Cyril's headmaster thought it advisable to send him home because public attention was catching up with him at school. Determined to put as good a face as she could on the situation, for the boy's sake, Constance took a box at the theatre and attended with Laura Hope the performance of *The Importance of Being Earnest*. Afterwards Constance took Cyril behind the scenes, where she heard, by chance that her husband and Alfred were putting a good face on things too. They had gone off together to Monte Carlo, after borrowing money from Ada Leverson's husband. The Marquess was remanded on £1,000 bail.

Before the trial of Queensberry, Robbie Ross called on Constance. He was on a delicate mission. He had always regarded her with a mixture of pity and admiration; and they had shared too, in the early days, a measure of jealousy of Alfred Douglas. But Robbie put all that behind him. The main thing was to clear Oscar's name of Queens-berry's charge. It would be good for Oscar in the eyes of public opinion, he pointed out, if she could find it in herself to have dinner with him and Douglas and then attend the theatre. She may well have flared up and thrown the Monte Carlo trip in his face—was that good for public opinion? And was her husband at last considering public opinion? Of course, Robbie would try to pacify her with the old story that to split with Alfred now was to fall into his father's hands. To continue in the usual manner would show that there was nothing to hide. On the other hand, Constance considered that a clean break and for Alfred to go abroad would be regarded by the public as a wise, circumspect move. All past resentments and humiliations were poured over Robbie's head, plus recriminations and temper on account of the future of her sons. And yet it was because of them that she in the end agreed to take part in the unbelievable charade.

Constance gave the performance of her life, making her way through the foyer of St James's Theatre on Oscar's arm, with Alfred Douglas, shining and fair, following behind. She was in white fur and Oscar elegant in a raven-blue opera cape. It was not every night that she was called upon to make a public appearance, to occupy a stage of her own, to act a melodrama, to be pilloried between Oscar and Alfred for all the world to see—not merely to see but to be indicated, even pointed at. A target for a barrage of opera glasses. For a woman of her sensitivity, it was excruciating.

At the interval Oscar left her with Alfred while he went to see the producer of *Earnest*, George Alexander. He should not, said George, have appeared until the case was over. And that, to Constance, was the first solid indication of what people thought the outcome would be.

When the charade was at an end, a cab was ordered. While handing her in, and before he gave the cabby instructions for Tite Street, Oscar told her that their fortune-teller, 'the Sybil of Mortimer street', had prophesied good things—and he needed money. Could she help? She was too far gone to regale him with his extravagances—Algiers, Monte Carlo, the Avondale, for she agreed to do what she could.

As one bent on a life-saving mission, Mrs Wilde, wife of the famous wit and dramatist, with two successful plays running at the same time, went borrowing. Her grandfather Lloyd did well in leaving her inheritance in trust, yet at a time like this she wished he had not. To borrow was humiliating—and yet, for Oscar's immediate legal fees, it was imperative. She got £50 from her cousin Eliza; Aunt Mary Napier loaned £150. No help could be expected from Aunts Emily or Carrie, so she went to Kensington, to Edward Burne-Jones—and left with another £150, to which she added £50 of what was left of her allowance. Robbie called for the money and promised to keep her informed at once of developments, for, because of the boys, she wanted to keep one jump ahead of the papers, for Vyvyan had now been sent home from his school because of the attitude of other boys.

The trial of Lord Queensberry on a charge of criminally libelling Oscar Wilde opened at the Old Bailey on 3rd April 1895. As the trial went on, the papers became more explicit about certain revelations which had come to light concerning a young man of Oscar's acquaintance.

"Did you ever kiss him?"

"Oh, dear no. He was a peculiarly plain boy . . ."

"Was that why you did not kiss him?"

Kisses, embraces, love letters, poems, presents—it was there in the Press for all the world to read. Constance was afraid for the innocence of Cyril and Vyvyan. She had need to be, for on the last day of the Queensberry libel case another letter was delivered by hand to Tite Street. It was from Oscar, expressly requesting that she allow no one in his rooms. Then, true to his word, Robbie Ross arrived from the Old Bailey to tell her what she already, in her heart, knew. The prosecution had been withdrawn, Queensberry was found not guilty of criminal libel, and there was a warrant issued for the arrest of her husband.

10

A Grotesque Nightmare

"Oscar Wilde arrested." So ran the headlines, so yelled the newsboys. There had been a delay of a few hours between the application for a warrant and the granting of it. In those few hours he could have fled the country, as many others did. But not Oscar. He stayed at the Cadogan Hotel with Robbie Ross, while Alfred Douglas raced to the House of Commons to see if a prosecution was inevitable. It was. At 6.30 Wilde heard the sound he had always dreaded. The footsteps of the policeman outside his door. The knock. The words. The arrest. Slightly drunk and dazed with an overwhelming sense of destiny, Constance's husband was taken to Bow Street police station, where he was charged and spent the night in the cells.

Laura Hope wrote in her diary for 5th April: "A most trying visit from Mrs. William Napier in a most frantic state about her poor niece Constance Wilde as the verdict has gone against her monstrous husband—the whole episode most terrible."

For Constance to have stayed at Tite Street was impossible. The House Beautiful was a marked place. Public opinion was already turning nasty, so she and the boys packed a few things and went to stay with Aunt Mary, leaving Arthur, the butler, to pay off the servants and look after the premises. From the haven of her aunt's house, Constance reviewed with a curious detachment, as though she were someone else, the fantastic furore, the never-ending nightmare, of the next few days. And while she could not eat or sleep, her cousin Eliza took charge of her sons. Although anxious herself, Eliza fussed over the boys and told them that their father was involved in some trouble but that all would be right presently, and would they play quietly and be good, and not bother mama?

On 9th April Laura Hope confided to her diary, "To the Napiers where I sat with poor Constance, the most miserable woman in London, I should think." If Eliza thought that "things would be right presently", the public at large were by no means confident that all would be right ever again.

There was a sudden dearth of aesthetic young men. There were letters to the Press ranging from the irate and indignant to the hostile and vitriolic. Jerome K. Jerome demanded, apart from Oscar's head, "the heads of the 500 noblemen of the world who shared Oscar Wilde's turpitude and so corrupt youth". At this stage Wilde could have dropped the action and sought obscurity in more liberal climes. The Prince of Wales, having been in numerous scrapes himself, was in no position publicly to defend his favourite dramatist. Young men who dared to appear in the streets with flowers, with elegance or with the slightest trace of effeminacy, were subject to jeers and referred to as 'Oscars'. Wilde's publishers withdrew copies of his books from shops, and George Alexander, who had not taken kindly to Oscar's appearance in his theatre with Constance and Lord Alfred, blackened out the name of the author of *The Importance of Being Earnest* from the hoardings outside his theatre.

Not everyone persisted in inhumanity. Henry James, in a letter to Edmund Gosse, wrote: ". . . the fall from nearly twenty years of a really unique kind of brilliant conspicuity (wit, art, conversation— one of our two or three dramatists) to that sordid prison cell and this gulf of obscenity over which the ghoulish public hangs and gloats, is beyond any utterance of irony or pang of compassion! He was never in the smallest degree interesting to me—but this hideous human history has made him so, in a manner."

Mrs Patrick Campbell with refreshing candour was heard to exclaim. "I don't care what they do, as long as they don't do it in the streets and frighten the horses!"

Surrounded by all this publicity, Aunt Mary Napier suspected that Cyril was becoming too inquisitive as to the kind of trouble his father was involved in. Displays on newspaper hoardings were difficult to dodge and even harder to explain. The boy was of an age not to be fobbed off with a trite answer, and so they packed him off to stay with Cousin Stanhope in Dublin until the trial was over.

Everything now hung on the trial, fixed for 26th April, many people of Constance's own class were uncertain how to regard her until the verdict was announced and were therefore markedly reserved. Others cut her dead in the streets, and some deliberately avoided her, which was worse. Opinion already was such that she dared not set foot in the Albemarle Club. The ordinary people in the streets terrified her. If she went out of doors, even briefly and veiled, they seemed to sense it and stared at the wife of Oscar Wilde as if she had developed two heads. Some pointed her out and shouted names; others hurled disgusting phrases. She was both astonished and overwhelmed at the amount of public vituperation which was unleashed. It was as though all the rumour and gossip of years had gathered to form one great eruption.

To escape all the unpleasantness and the hounding of the Press, she fled on 19th April to stay with her beloved 'Mia Madre' at Babbacombe Cliff. From her haven of safety she forced herself to follow the coverage of the trial in the papers—not only the English but the Continental papers. It helped her to discuss it with Lady Mount Temple, who understood and talked without embarrassment. It had been impossible for Constance to talk to her Aunt Mary and Eliza; they were too near and feared to mention Oscar's name at all, except in hushed whispers, and to her face they referred to herself as "Poor, dear Constance". It was not only the air at Babbacombe which was refreshing.

'Dorian Gray' and other "passages suggestive of corruption" were attacked and plugged by the prosecuting counsel, and for three days all the evidence produced or threatened by the Queensberry defence at the earlier trial was repeated and followed up by hordes of unreliable witnesses. Constance waited for the verdict with all the apprehension of a first night, for on the verdict of those twelve jurors hung her future, her fate. But the jury could not agree. If Oscar's name had not been linked with that of Alfred Taylor, the jury might have returned a 'Not Guilty' verdict, but as Taylor had already appeared before the courts and was known to be one of the infamous Fitzroy Street boys—one of the two who, when the club was raided in August, was discovered in a yellow taffeta gown and frilly petticoats—the jury could not reach agreement.

A new trial was fixed for 20th May, and Oscar, this time, was bailed out to the tune of £5,000 raised by the Reverend Stewart Headlam—whose socialism and unorthodoxy had cost him his place in the church—and Percy, Lord Douglas of Hawick, who was Bosie's elder brother.

Following this good news came a telegram from Eliza to urge Constance to return to town, as the creditors, hearing a whisper of bankruptcy, were on the rampage. Travelling up at once, Constance entered the house by the back door, for the sight of Mrs Wilde at the front might have started a mad rush. She collected her clothes and those of the boys, her treasured Dante and Petrarch, the travelling bookcase and the crimson, leather-bound visitors' book which had been given to her at their house-warming. The book which had seen the beginning now saw the end. Famous names, friends, celebrities, poets, they would never come to the House Beautiful again. She may well have read, as though it were the last rites, the poem on the front page, written in Oscar's beautifully formed handwriting and entitled 'To my Wife':

> I can write no stately proem
> as a prelude to my lay;
> From a poet to a poem
> I would dare to say
>
> For if of these fallen petals
> One to you seem fair;
> Love will waft it till it settles
> On your hair.
>
> And when winds and winter harden
> All the loveless land,
> It will whisper of the garden,
> You will understand.

Was it prophetic? The winter had hardened; and as for understanding, was it possible to understand with so much of her life in ruins what had driven her brilliant husband to cast everything in the mire? Soon the yellow and dove-grey staircase would echo to the cry of the auctioneer, and the bailiffs would be entertaining the mob. The House Beautiful would be open to the avid gaze of the masses, the cruel mentality of the collective bunch; giggling shop girls would be touching her draperies and silk hangings; and hectoring young men in tight collars, gesticulating, swaggering, vulgar and distasteful. If the literati of ten years earlier thought the house "vaguely sinful and bizarre", what construction would those of the tight collars put on it? Soon, philistine hands would desecrate Oscar's beautifully bound first editions, many priceless, her exquisite embroideries, the fort in the nursery, Vyvyan's large box of toys.

She hurriedly thanked Arthur, who had dismissed the servants according to her instructions; they had been loyal to the end and were paid out of her allowance. She had settled with what tradespeople she could, and promised to pay the rest in time. Arthur too was paid out of her own pocket. Poor man, he had been with the Wildes all their married life and was very fond of them and frantic about their future. Perhaps the butler and mistress exchanged the usual platitudes which serve to cover a hurtful situation.

"Let me know where you are . . ."

"Yes ma'am."

"For after the trial, Mr Wilde and I shall be looking—"

"Yes, Mrs Oscar . . ."

Voices trailed, and sentences remained unfinished, as uncertain as the hopes they tried to convey. The Chatelaine of the House Beautiful had left it for ever. Deprived of the right to her home after ten years, she returned to Aunt Mary Napier and Eliza. Meanwhile, the cab in which Oscar had left prison had been chased through the town by a gang of Queensberry's prize-fighters. Every hotel had refused him entrance because of the bullies, and eventually, hunted down like a weary fox, he had taken refuge at his mother's house in Oakley Street. Constance knew he would be miserable there, for he never got on well with his brother. She wanted to see him, but not in Oakley Street. This was no time to face 'Speranza's' theatricals, or Willie's hysteria, or her sister-in-law.

After a day or two Ada Leverson rescued Oscar and took him to stay with her and her husband, Ernest, until the second trial in three weeks time. The reportage of the Queensberry trial had caused such a public outcry that the Leversons felt obliged to offer their servants a month's salary if they preferred not to wait upon her guest. Not one of them took up the option, and all declared that they were proud to wait upon "poor Mr Wilde". People were good to him. Not the populace, but individuals such as the actress Mrs Bernard Beere, Lady Dorothy Neville, Will Rothenstein and men of the calibre of Asquith and Haldane. Constance, knowing the mentality of her relatives, was relieved that his fate did not turn on their outlook.

While the Leversons' servants were proud to wait upon "poor Mr Wilde", poor Mrs Wilde, feeling like a child who had overspent its pocket money, pleaded with the Lloyd family solicitor, Mr Hargrove, to advance her some of her allowance. She must have money, she insisted; whatever the outcome of the second trial, she must have money to act as she thought fit. Mr Hargrove, sensing determination and having sympathy for the situation she found herself in, agreed to solve at least the financial aspect.

Friends were urging Oscar to make his getaway as others had, but Lady Wilde's advice had been that he should stand trial and not "do the dishonourable thing". Constance visited him at the Leversons', risking the glare of the publicity she shunned, to add her voice to theirs, to urge him to skip his bail and go to France, where she was prepared to take the children to join him. That she was ready to do this, to take up her life with him again after the awful disclosures which would have shocked most Victorian wives out of their wits, is understandable only when the fact that she was not merely an ordinary Victorian wife is taken into consideration. She had been as aesthetic as her husband; she was used to extravagant relationships, to the company of artists and literary folk, to high-flown conversation; she had grown with it and got used to it. Her husband, she had known, was shocking Society by 'posing' as Queensberry had put it. To discover that it was no pose was indeed a severe shock, and the threat of discovery was no doubt worse than discovery itself, but the bond between Oscar and his wife was always there, and one can detect in their later relationship something of the mother-and-child syndrome. Her protective instinct toward Oscar had been heightened by the attitude of her relations. She had defended her husband against all comers, and now that he had his back to the wall, her loyalty came to the top. She could no longer defend him, but if flight was the answer, she was prepared to go. With the influence of Alfred Douglas gone, she hoped something could be salvaged, something rebuilt out of the ruins of their marriage. Of course there were a hundred different things to think of concerning the future, and all was vain speculation, for everything depended on whether Oscar would leave the country, and if he did not, everything would depend on the outcome of the trial, the third trial. How adaptable her nature had become; but how far, and to what extent, would it adapt further?

She had not seen Oscar since the nightmare evening of being

pilloried between him and Alfred Douglas at the theatre. He had lost surplus weight, which suited him; he was impeccably dressed, with the inevitable flower in his buttonhole, which was, according to Ada, delivered every day. The hairdresser too called daily. Apart from lines of tiredness and worry, he looked more like the man she had married than the man he had become. Being naturally affectionate, almost extravagantly so, there would be a holding-out and clasping of hands, and an embrace in which Oscar murmured his sorrow for the hurt and shame he had brought upon her and the boys. This was her moment to break away, to keep her composure and urge him to leave the country. She would have done well to quote from *Lady Windermere's Fan*, where Mrs Chevely says of approaching scandal, "Think of their loathesome joy, of the delight they would have of dragging you down, of the mud an the mire they would plunge you in. Think of the hypocrite, of his greasy smile, writing articles, arranging foulness the public's pleasure." He would not agree to go, even for the sake of his sons. He was afraid he would be seized by the police before he even got to Dover—and what headlines that would make! As for Cyril and Vyvyan, they would think badly of him as it was, but to have skipped bail, to have fled, to have acted the coward, would be worse. Constance could sense 'Speranza' behind all the arguments he put up. She had seen the set of his face, a face she knew better than anyone else, and could see, with fear and frustration, that he was preparing himself for the final act of the drama, his self-appointed role of martyr. He had always admitted to a sense of tragedy; it was the only thing left untasted. Oh, how well she knew this husband of hers. Perhaps it was because she knew him too well that it was impossible for her to be other than she was. Tragedy was the only thing left, and he was determined to sample it.

Towards the end of May Oscar Wilde was brought before the court at the Old Bailey yet again. The newsboys ran in the street shouting the name of Wilde. The placards and the air were thick with con- demnation already, and reading the newspapers brought a sense of doom. How was it possible for the ordinary man in the street, such as the jury, not to be deeply shocked at the revelations? She feared the little minds of the jury. The masses were, as Oscar said in court, "shocked beyond their highest expectations!" But still, there was room for hope, for Queensberry's witnesses, whom he had hired, had been proved unreliable. Each day dragged interminably on. Between heart-quaking alarms and vile fantasies of her husband with Douglas, between the agony of waiting and the fear of knowing, she knew that, whatever abysmal maze he had let himself into, she would always love him. On the last day the Napiers' servant came hot-foot from the crowded gallery of the Old Bailey. The verdict was that of 'Guilty'.

The judge had said, "That you, Wilde, have been the centre of a circle of corruption of the most hideous kind among men, it is impossible to doubt. I shall, under the circumstances, be expected to pass the severest sentence that the law allows. In my judgement it is totally inadequate for such a case as this. The sentence of the court is that you be imprisoned and kept to hard labour for two years."

Queensberry had been at the back of this terrible indictment. Oh, how she had come to hate that family. It was common knowledge that a lot of the evidence had been trumped up by the Marquess and that there were those who reckoned that the charges should never have been laid against Oscar. How loathsome the words were, and—thinking of Mrs Chevely in *Lady Windermere's Fan*—how they had delighted to bring him down! How the article writers had arranged the foulness for the public pleasure. Like Oscar's poem about the "winter hardening", Mrs Chevely's words could be called prophetic. Constance's husband, famous as he was, had poked fun at their Victorian society. He had conducted himself in an unconventional and unnatural manner. He had strayed from convention, and it had turned on him—he who had been so gifted . . . so fascinating . . . the most fascinating member of a fascinating family. What price, she thought bitterly, what price fascination now? And what would become of Oscar? How would he, or could he, face up to life in prison? Having thought of him, what of the boys? That their father was in prison was an enormity which she was only just beginning to realize. One thing was certain: they must not know. They must never know. Then she thought of herself and felt that life had cheated her. Happiness was gone, and on the whole there had been so little of it. Her life "seemed to be cut to pieces as her hand was by its lines". She felt as though Oscar were dead and that for the present she was dead too, for without him what kind of life was there? True, some of it had been a weariful succession of wakeful dawns and lonely nights. There was no peace and no joy in love despoiled. Yet, in unshared torment, she loved him . . . could not love him less for what he had become. And always her thoughts came full circle. Back to Oscar.

The terrible catastrophe was too near as yet for her to pick anything out of it. Her actions, her future and that of the children had depended on the result of the trial—and prepared as she was for what the verdict might be, it still came as a crushing blow. But people survived catastrophes. She would survive. The future must be devoted to the children, hers and Oscar's.

Disturbing news came in a telegram from Cousin Stanhope. Cyril was very upset about his father. He had seen certain words on placards connected with his father's name and, by looking them up, discovered the nature of the charges. Added to that, people in Dublin knew who he was and were busy re-telling old scandals as well as discussing this new one. Poor Cyril, he was going on twelve now and his childhood spoiled and tainted. And when he arrived in London? Would it be any better than Dublin? What about school? The boys would be targets for the taunts of bullies and ruffians. More calmly now, Constance surveyed the elements of survival. She had condemned flight in the aftermath of discovery; but now it was not merely a consideration but a necessity. There would be no peace for the sons of Oscar Wilde.

Constance decided first of all to stay in Switzerland with her brother, Otho, where, away from the notoriety which surrounded the name of Wilde, she would be able to gather herself to more rational thought. Apart from Otho and his family, the Ranee lived on the Italian border, and Princess Alice in Monaco. Carlos and Caroline Blacker—who had provided part of the financial backing for *Lady Windermere's Fan*—lived in Freiburg.

Cyril was not too keen on going away again when he had only just come back from Ireland, but seeing that he knew about his father, Constance was able to explain that she had to stay in England a little longer "to see if anything can be done for your poor papa" and that she would join them presently. But first she had to find a suitable governess. The only one the agency could produce at such short notice was a French woman; "very religious, and therefore most reliable" was the commendation. Time was short, and all Constance needed the woman for was to take the boys safely to Switzerland and to stay with them until she arrived. Mademoiselle certainly seemed capable of that. Another thing in her favour was that, being recently come from France and of a meditative nature, she had no idea who her charges were. As for prayers, Constance no doubt was of the opinion that they could all do with a few.

What a dreadful indictment on the Society of the period that Constance, distraught and desolate, was forced to send her children out of the country away from public opinion. Although they were in the charge of a complete stranger and being whisked away from all that was secure and solid and familiar, it was better than their young lives being blighted by scandal. Having gone through the upheaval of being hounded from their schools, driven out of their home to stay with relatives and deprived of their father, they had to cope without their mother, just when they needed her most. It was especially hard for Cyril because he knew the nature of the charges brought against his father—a secret he shared with his mother. But at least he understood the reason for their hurried departure, whereas Vyvyan—who remained in complete ignorance about his father's offence until his late teens—must have spent hours of childish agony wondering what it was all about.

The governess was a grim and slightly hysterical woman who was bored with children and avoided their company as often as possible, either to pray or to write letters. She left the boys locked in their hotel room in Paris while she went out with her friends and gave them neither books to read nor anything to play with, still less a decent meal. They were booked into the Hotel du Righi-Vaudois under their own name of Wilde when they reached Glion, and this being their destination, things looked up a little. They had beautiful countryside in which to play, and they made friends with two old sisters who were Russian countesses living in the hotel. They were extremely kind to the boys and gave them sweets and stamps, and tea out of a samovar.

When the boys were taken to Glion, their father was taken to Pentonville Prison, and their mother sorted out her muddled affairs as best she could. Whatever belongings they had were to be forwarded, for as she had never returned to Ely Place after her grandmother's funeral, so she felt she would never live in England again. The House Beautiful was no longer theirs. The sale had stripped it bare, and there was so much owing that the suspected bankruptcy was now fully declared. There were arrangements to be made with the family solicitor, and she thanked God for Grandfather Lloyd's financial wisdom; had her legacy been arranged otherwise, either Oscar would have gone through it or the creditors would have scooped it all, and she and the children would have been left paupers, at the mercy of the family. She shuddered at the thought and reckoned that it was possible to educate and provide for her sons on £1,000 a year, for living on the Continent was much cheaper than in England.

While going about her arrangements Constance did not know which was harder to bear, the cruelty or the kindness of people.

Richard Haldane, one of the 'Souls', in particular was haunted by the thought of a man of Oscar's sensitivity going through the soul-destroying process of hard labour. Not only that, but to be deprived of any book, save the Bible, a prayer book and a hymn book. To be allowed one letter in three months, and no visits until the same time had elapsed, and then only one visit per three months, seemed callous in the extreme. Richard Haldane promised Constance that he would visit Oscar in his Parliamentary capacity and take news from time to time to Lady Wilde. Other eminent people tried to minimize the harsh sentence with campaigns and petitions, but such was public opinion that Constance felt that all their efforts would be in vain.

Before she left London, Robert Sherard, whom she had met on her honeymoon in Paris, and about whose resemblance to the poet Chatterton the newly married couple had made great play, was one of the first to rally round his old friend, followed by the demure Robbie Ross. Constance knew that Robbie's manner of life was the same as Oscar's and Alfred Douglas's. The knowledge had somehow been conveyed over the past two or three years—conveyed, suspected, but not admitted. And yet she liked the little Canadian and hated Alfred, because, unlike the latter, he had not tried to take Oscar from her. As for Robert Sherard, she doubted if he subscribed to the same club. He had what she called a puritanically shaped mouth and over the years had lost a lot of his charm. As for Alfred Douglas, Constance had never hated anyone more, for while she survived the ruin he had brought about, he was safely tucked away in the south of France, more resentful of not having got the better of the father he hated than sorrowful for having put Oscar in prison. Lucifer! Devil! That persuading smile, petulant toss of his golden head, radiant personality, so beautiful, engaging, enslaving. He had bewitched her husband as surely as the Wildes had bewitched her.

If the Wildes had bewitched her, the spell was still unbroken, for in Mr Hargrove's mahogany and frosted-glass office she had refused to sever her connections. So she told both him and Adrian Hope, whom Aunt Mary Napier thought a good adviser, being a distant relative and the nearest man in the family, that she would not agree to a divorce. Nor would she entertain any notion of changing her name. She was utterly determined not to accede to any of their well-meaning requests. They hoped to rush her and crowd her into doing something she would later regret. They wanted to get everything settled and cleared up, and all unfortunate connections severed. Knowing that they would try again, and anxious to avoid pressure from her well-meaning aunts, also to avoid the publicity of being Mrs Oscar Wilde, she assembled her things and fled to join her sons.

On the way to the boat-train, at Euston Station, she saw through the cab window the theatre hoardings bearing her husband's name slashed and painted over. Bookshops had withdrawn every book by the author, even the fairy tales. It was as though the name of Wilde was an excrescence. And although for years she had been living with a presentiment of some disaster, the realization of it surpassed even the Somerset scandal.

Before leaving her aunt's house, a letter was delivered to her. It was about their faithful butler, Arthur. He had committed suicide. She was horrified, and wondered at the reason behind it. Could it be that he was worried about employment, for who would employ him knowing he had been in service at the house of Oscar Wilde? Then came the awful doubt. Had he and Oscar. . . ? Was he afraid that the police would winkle him out? After all, Somerset had been found in the arms of his footman. Was there to be no end to the repercussions? And it had been revealed at the trials that Oscar had been friends with . . . come, Constance, she would admonish herself, you must face up to it; he had not merely been friends with but had kissed and caressed . . . and loved clerks, telegraph boys. Poor Arthur, whatever the reason for his suicide, it had been committed as a direct result of having been in service with the Wildes. She hoped it was not an omen.

Constance travelled in late May from Dover to Calais, by train to Paris and then made another sixteen-hour journey to Geneva, changing trains to Montreux, followed by a drive then to Territet and the funicular railway from there to Glion. A quiet, unobtrusive, uncommunicative English lady, she was one of the many tourists travelling at that time of the year with the assistance of Thomas Cook Ltd.

Her back, injured in a fall downstairs some months earlier, was still giving her trouble, and she arrived at the hotel in gathering dusk looking forward to a rest after being re-united with her scamps. But what did she find? The boys still playing about outside and the governess in her room, entirely ignorant as to where her charges were and what they were up to.

Naturally, Constance was angry at this gross incompetence. She immediately took the surprised governess to task, and signs that she had neglected her duty were not hard to find. One can imagine the children's version of the situation and what a tale they would pour into the ears of their outraged parent. All the indignities and hardships they had suffered at the hands of the unfeeling governess, all the injustices and unfairnesses would be aired, leaving Constance in no doubt that the French woman had outlived her usefulness—at least, as far as the Wildes were concerned. To the relief and delight of Cyril and Vyvyan, she was dismissed at once, and they had their darling mama to themselves again.

Being reconciled with her sons, however, brought its own problems and pain, for inevitably Vyvyan would ask the dreaded question, "Where is papa?" There was nothing else could be done except to tell him, with a glance at the silent Cyril, that his father was still in England and would join them when his business was finished. He would then want to know about his box of toys and their fort. Poor Constance, she could not possibly tell him about an item in the catalogue of the Tite Street sale which read, "Lot 237 a large quantity of toys". It was at moments like this when her anger and frustration would veer from Alfred Douglas to their father, whose weakness had deprived two little boys of their favourite soldiers and fort.

Almost three months had passed since the Black Maria had taken Oscar to Pentonville Prison, and according to regulations he was, after this time, allowed to send and receive a letter; also he was entitled to a twenty-minute visit from a friend. Alfred Douglas had applied to the Governor for permission to write, but Oscar declined in favour of Constance. Alfred was most put out; he could scarcely believe Oscar preferred to "write to his family rather than me"! Constance, too, was becoming anxious at the lack of communication; she had not seen Oscar since the interview at Ada Leverson's house, and wanted to let him know she and the boys were well, for he was completely in the dark. He would also think she was going ahead with the divorce proceedings which had been first mooted when he was committed. Her surmise was correct, for Lily Wilde, Willie's wife, had informed him that she believed it to be so. Lily got her letter through on compassionate grounds: ". . . as I am expecting my confinement shortly, and one's life is always more or less in danger, perhaps you would relax the rule, and if so, would you give him my fondest love and say how often I think of him and long to see him, also, what perhaps will give him the most pleasure, that his mother is wonderfully well."

Constance was not as free an agent as Lily, for the solicitor, Mr Hargrove, and Adrian Hope had insisted, in her own interests and those of her sons, that she was to contact her husband only through them. Otho, her dear, dependable brother, was proving himself to be a positive brick; he had the ideal but clandestine solution. Mr Hargrove had said nothing about Otho not writing to his brother-in-law! This he did, informing the prisoner of their whereabouts and assuring him of Constance's love and forgiveness. Meanwhile, Oscar's letter via the solicitor had crossed hers in the post. So delicate was the subject that Mr Hargrove travelled all the way to Switzerland to present his client with the letter. It was the most touching and penitent letter the lawyer had ever seen—and he must have set eyes on many. Completely won over, he backed down from persuading her to petition for divorce and suggested that, on Oscar's release, she and the boys could join him and make a fresh start—on the other side of the world! Otho was not quite so extreme: he considered France or Spain would do.

Robert Sherard had been Oscar's first visitor, but Constance applied through the Prison Commission to be allowed a visit due to the exceptional domestic circumstances. Arrangements were then made for the Wilde children to stay with their uncle and his family while their mother travelled to England in the company of a family friend, a Miss Boxwell, whose holiday was over and consequently she was returning to London where she lived.

The little colony of English people—there always seemed to be one—were pleasant enough, and the anonymity of being merely another tourist was a relief from being pointed out as "There goes the wife of Oscar Wilde." Veiled hats, which had been a feature of her life since the Queensberry trial, were now left in the hatbox. Yet the past could not be dismissed in a hurry. The Countesses' room, darkened with fringed hangings and littered with urns and ikons, would remind her of her mother-in-law's house in Oakley Street; and the way the old ladies continually rolled and smoked cigarettes reminded her of Madame Blavatsky and how Oscar had chaffed her on the relative merits of Theosophy and Aestheticism.

Otho Holland, who lived in Bevaix with his second wife and family, arrived a few days later to talk things over with his sister and see what was to be done. His bland, scholastic approach to the subject of her ordeal was a marvellous and calming contrast to the hysteria of the

London family.

Otho returned to his home in Bevaix leaving his sister and the boys to enjoy another few weeks of the Swiss summer. It was not to last. Scandal caught up with them. News travelled slowly, but travel it did. The hotel manager, having realized who she was, asked her to leave. A hurried telegram to Otho brought the anticipated visit to Bevaix forward; and Constance, with children, portmanteaus, boxes, trunks and travelling rugs, continued her travels like the itinerant tinkers she had seen wandering about in Ireland.

Otho and his family lived on the top floor of a two-storey chalet near Lake Neuchâtel in the wine-making province of Switzerland. There Constance met her sister-in-law for the first time. Her brother's second wife was a quiet, kindly, housewifely body, who clearly did not know what to make of her husband's beautiful sister, who sometimes walked with a limp and was at the hub of a fearful scandal.

There was still two weeks before the trip to England, and while staying at Bevaix Otho pointed out to his sister the wisdom of changing her name. Even if she could withstand the ignominy, it was not fair to submit the children to it; they would soon be attending school, and did she want a repetition of the unkindness shown in England? Of course she did not. Constance was persuaded. The name chosen was that of her brother, the family name of Holland. Having convinced herself it was the correct thing, indeed the only thing, to do, it was quite another matter to explain and convince Vyvyan and Cyril of the necessity. Otho was nothing if not thorough. He had all the documents to hand, and the actual signing of them was a solemn affair.

With the aid of a pen, Constance killed off the name she had been so proud and happy to take twelve years before at St James's Church, Sussex Gardens, she in her gown of cowslip yellow and Speranza in bright red, and Oscar making jokes about a full house. She had become on that fine day in early summer Mrs Oscar Wilde, for better—or worse. Now she was to be known as Constance Mary Holland. With a few strokes of the pen, the deed was done.

Vyvyan was unfortunate in having more to remove than the others. Apart from changing his last name, he had to alter the spelling of his first to the more commonplace Vivian. The only satisfaction derived from the melancholy business of the change-over was the fact that Constance had made the decision herself without pressure from her solicitor.

It was the middle of September when Constance was free to set out to London. The weather was mellow, and cool enough to make travelling comfortable. Miss Boxwell must have been a pleasant companion and a comfort. She was obviously someone Constance knew well and with whom she could discuss the ordeal which lay ahead, for ordeal it would certainly be. She had written to Sherard about the visit, and he, being Oscar's first visitor, had tried to prepare her for the worst. On her arrival in London on Saturday, the longed-for permission was awaiting her at Miss Boxwell's apartment on the top floor of the Metropolitan Industrial Dwellings, Holbein House, where she was staying. Naturally, Constance did not want anyone to know of her presence in town and was adamant about not seeing anyone at all—apart from Robert Sherard, that is. He was invited to call on Tuesday, no doubt to discuss her meeting with Oscar on the Monday.

The terrible strain of the Holland-Wilde change-over had now given way—as though her mind were never to be free—to a reflective anxiety on her relationship with her husband. Such reflections had not arisen while Mr Hargrove was in opposition to a reconciliation. But now that his opposition was lifted and she was free to make a new life with Oscar, she was forced to face the question of her emotions toward him. Emotions there certainly were. He was not a man one could look at without having some immediate emotive response. Were her feelings those of concern? Loyalty? The sinned-against for the sinner? Feelings of protection? Or was it a mixture of them all? And did this mixture amount to love? And were these sufficient to sustain a future together? Further, would the future be different from the past? Question after question presented itself until she was not sure whether it was love at all—or merely a haunting.

Despite Robert Sherard's warning, nothing could have prepared her for the horrors of visiting day at Wandsworth Prison. Noticeably conspicuous on account of her fashionable and well-cut clothes, she was the object of curious eyes. Apprehensive lest they guessed her identity, pushed and jostled by the crowds, she was distressed already, knowing how Oscar, so gentle and civilized, humane and cultivated, must be suffering. The bell sounded. The crowd surged into the visiting area, and Constance went through with them like a marionette. The waiting area had been bad enough, but the zoo-like aspect of the visiting room was infinitely worse. A grill of three feet separated prisoner and visitor. Those who had been before soon negotiated the object of their visit and were busy discussing their affairs across the gap. Her eyes roamed the barriers, trying not to look as though it was her first time in case officers asked who she was looking for, and then voices would be raised above babble shouting for Wilde! That was to be avoided at all costs. Feeling overwhelmed and sick and breathless, she tried to smile and keep dry-eyed at the sight of the big man looking awkward in shapeless grey prison clothes. His face was ashen, and he looked ill. Whatever they said had to be in raised voices to cover the gap. She told Sherard afterwards:

It was indeed awful, more so than I had any conception it could be. I could not touch him. I scarcely spoke. . . . When I go again I am to get at the Home Secretary through Mr. Haldane and try to get a room to see him in and touch him again. He has been mad these last three years, and he says that if he saw Alfred Douglas he would kill him. So he had better keep away and be satisfied with having marred a fine life. Few people can boast of so much.

Constance was not returning to Bevaix, for, at sixteen hundred feet above sea level, the winter was too severe for her constitution and the lumbar condition which was not improving; to make matters worse, the arm which had taken her weight as she fell down the stairs was also becoming affected. Her friend the Ranee had found an apartment at Sori, on the coast, which was only a couple of miles from her own villa. The apartment was big enough to take Otho and his family, and in that manner she intended to spend the winter months.

While travelling back to the Continent, Constance had a lot to think about. It would be another three months before a letter could pass between her and Oscar, and there was so much to be discussed, the upheaval of a lifetime to sort out. Then the thought came to nag. What if well-meaning people interfered between her and Oscar? It was far too expensive to make this journey every three months, but others, those in London, would be seeing him. Robbie Ross, for instance, would need to see him about the bankruptcy proceedings—and Robert Sherard. She wished there was no one between them. No solicitors. No well-meaning friends on his side, and family on her side. There was an understanding between her and Oscar. She now had his complete trust—and she treasured it and was jealous of it. Already she was feeling the encroaching frustration. What if her or his instructions were not executed properly? She being in Italy and he in prison, they were vulnerable and at anyone's mercy.

11

Exile

Sori was a quiet little fishing village, set in a valley and spanned by a massive viaduct which carried the coastal railway from Genoa to La Spezia and then on to Rome. The Hollands, as they were now called, rented the villa obtained for them by the Ranee, which was perched high above the village, with a garden stretching down to a low cliff and a ramshackle flight of steps which in turn led to the sea-shore. It was an exciting place for children; there were quicksands on the beach; a firework factory a couple of miles away, which occasionally blew up; the fishing fleet down in the village, and the frightening experience of the midday express thundering along the viaduct.

Constance's apartment compared badly to the House Beautiful; its Swiss-Italian décor was plain and efficiently spacious . . . there was no overmantel by Donoghue . . . no Japanese sofa, silken hangings . . . and no box of toys. And poor Oscar locked up in that hideous place. She railed at and reviled bitterly the name of Alfred Douglas. Because Alfred was free. Because he had so wantonly encouraged Oscar to bring that terrible lawsuit against his father. Of course, she now knew full well the manner of life Oscar had been leading; but she could not relate, and never would, the depravity outlined in the papers to the father of her children. Never in a thousand years could she put him on the level of the likes of the Fitzroy Street boys. She considered he must have been mad. There was no other explanation.

What with her husband in prison, the stiffness in her back, the uselessness of her fingers, the education of the boys going to pieces—and the Italian bread, which did not agree with her digestion, which since Oscar's trial had not been robust, everything seemed too much. After a while, Constance pulled herself together. Two years would soon pass, Robert Sherard had said, and six months were gone already.

In February 1896 Constance received a letter from her sister-in-law. It contained news of the birth of a daughter, and Willie was delighted. They were calling the child Dorothy Irene. What Lily Wilde did not mention in her letter was that, through the Leversons, Oscar had borrowed £50 to pay for the confinement because Willie had no money. Another incident concerning Mrs Willie is that, while Oscar was taking refuge at Oakley Street from Queensberry's bullies, she had begged him to leave his American fur coat there for safe keeping. Robert Sherard had since written and called to collect it but, receiving no answer, presumed it had been pawned or sold. The main point, and the reason for the letter, was to say that Lady Wilde had died of a chill following bronchitis. "Oscar has not yet been informed. I await your instructions."

Constance at once telegraphed instructions that he was not to be told by anyone but herself. The news saddened her . . . 'Speranza', Isola's tall and strikingly beautiful mother . . . by the ice rink worrying over Willie . . . gliding across Merrion Square dressed in black and yellow silk to sign the Home Rule Roll . . . queening it over her salon. And, on a more intimate note, she and Sir William sitting before the fire in their drawing-room, the walls cluttered with books and glass-fronted cases of glistening carp; he reading poetry and never having a more appreciative audience than she. Unlike Constance, when trouble and scandal came, Lady Wilde, even before the outcome of Sir William's trial, went about her affairs with a regality that did not recognize public opinion. Constance's dear mother-in-law, was now indeed "above the miasmas of the commonplace". Despite the weather, despite her spinal trouble, she was determined to travel to London.

At the railway station at Genoa, Otho saw his sister comfortably seated in a compartment. The porters raced along the platform, slamming doors, yelling for the train to be cleared. Otho stood on the platform, hand raised in a formal gesture, hat in hand; a solid, reliable figure in her changing world.

The palm trees of the Ligurian coast merged into the fir trees of the Swiss winter, bearing Constance through the St Gotthard tunnel on her arduous journey to England. There were not many people travelling, so that the guards and porters were able to attend to her every comfort, and of course there was plenty of time for thought. She intended to make the most of this visit. It would be much more tolerable, for before leaving Sori she had written to Richard Haldane, asking if she could break this delicate and melancholy piece of news to her husband in the privacy of a private room and not in the hideous cage affair with warders and the world looking on. Oscar had been transferred, now that the bankruptcy proceedings were over, to Reading Gaol.

On approaching the prison, she thought it more grim, if anything, than Wandsworth. A forlorn and vulnerable figure against the formidable massiveness of the prison gates, she rang the bell for admittance; a small door in the gate opened at once, like a hungry mouth, and she was swallowed. The jaws closed. The officer on duty, informed of her likely appearance, took her, with a civility not afforded before, to his superior, who told her that the Governor had granted the concession and would she follow him to what was called the Solicitor's Room. She arranged herself behind the heavy-legged mahogany table and waited, listening to keys jangling, feet trampling and silence as they stopped outside the door.

On her last visit there had been too much clamour, noise and embarrassment, plus the three feet of designated space between them. This time she would have to brace herself for the impact of that first intimate scrutiny. Eyes riveted on the door, she was determined not to raise her veil until the first impression of the sight of him had passed, for if his appearance was shocking in any way, she did not want him to see a reflection of it in her eyes.

The door opened. Her husband was standing between two warders. He did not step forward into the room until he was told. She was glad of the veil, for although they said he was well, he looked ill. She was momentarily stunned. His hair, once waved and thick to the collar line, was cropped. His face, always pale, was sallow and haggard. Eyes, once so lively with expressive amusement, were lustreless. The dejected forward stoop of his broad shoulders and the grey prison clothes completed the pitiable sight of a man slowly going to pieces.

She had wanted the privacy of a room, "to touch him again". There would be the embrace, and tears, his and hers. He was ashamed of his hands, stained and coarse with oakum picking, his nails broken and dirty. He was ashamed to stand in such a state before her and, observing, that she too was not in good health, was overwhelmed that she should have travelled so far, in appalling February weather, to break the news of his mother's death herself.

He was still fond of his wife and stricken to have brought shame on her and his sons. That she was standing by him, she who had known and loved him before any of his male lovers, helped him to hang on to reality. Her letter, clean against Hargrove's instructions, and her reiterated forgiveness proved her loyalty—a loyalty which he had betrayed.

Wilde had often said, in those last years when he had become bored with marriage, that she did not understand him, as though that were reason and excuse to jettison his responsibilities and indulge himself. And since when has understanding been a thing to claim as of right? Constance could very well have echoed the same sentiment. He was later to say of the visit that his wife had been kind and gentle and sweet to him. In the hour made available they discussed their affairs. Although not proceeding with the divorce—in the preparation of which the name of the witness on whom Hargrove relied was none other than the Oxford servant whom Alfred Douglas had insisted Oscar take into service at Worthing—they were advised to obtain a judicial separation, this being necessary to safeguard their children from being 'orphaned' in the event of her death. An appointment of a guardian followed on this. Mr Hargrove had suggested Adrian Hope, and although Oscar did not care for the appointment of someone so against him, he agreed. They both knew that Hope would guard the children's legal interests; and in such an unfortunate event taking place, Constance knew that her Cousin Eliza and Aunt Mary Napier would supply the love and care. Oscar begged her not to spoil Cyril as Lady Queensberry had spoiled Alfred Douglas. She told him that both boys sent their love and knew that she had come to tell their papa of his mother's death. They talked about schools and of Carlos Blacker inviting her to Heidelberg, where there were many schools to choose from, and how in Germany Oscar's books, far from being banned, were used as textbooks for English language subjects. It was highly unlikely that their identity would be discovered, but if it were, there would not be the same distressing scandal as in England.

While in prison, Oscar had more than enough time to reflect with searing pain on the events which had brought him and Constance face to face under such grim conditions. He was filled with a bitter remorse to have brought shame and unhappiness to his wife and the children whom he dearly loved, and who in turn idolized their beloved papa. He told her there were children in Reading Gaol about the same age as his own. He was tremendously touched by their plight, knowing the cruelty that was practised by day and night and the frustration of not being able to help. One little fellow was so small that there were not clothes to fit him. Oscar was shocked by the barbarous system of locking children up in dark cells; he could not bear to hear their sobbing at night for their parents and was terrified lest one of the sterner kind of warders heard and beat them.

Time was running out, and very little was left to talk about the marriage settlement, Oscar's share of which was mixed up with the Official Receiver. In the absence of his friend Robbie Ross, who was ill, Constance was the one he could trust. If necessary she would communicate with Ross, for he and Sherard were the only friends of Oscar's for whom she now had any regard. She had resented Robbie Ross at first, but when he had joined her in the wings, having been edged from the centre of the stage of Oscar's life to make room for 'the Golden Boy', he had become a kind of ally.

The allotted visiting time had expired. The discussion had ended, and all the things that could never be said were uttered in the last kiss, the final embrace. Like a marionette, Oscar jumped to the command of the warders and was marched out. He did not look back.

While still in London Constance had insisted that Oscar, in the event of her death, should maintain a third share of the marriage settlement. If it was left to her family, Oscar would not, she knew, get a penny of Grandfather Lloyd's money. She did not intend him and the boys ever to be destitute.

Having rested a few days Constance began the journey back to Italy. It was raining heavily and was bitterly cold, and the Channel looked far from inviting. The crossing was slow and rough, and her digestion, being far from robust, stood no chance against the heaving swell.

From Calais she travelled second class to Paris, spent a night in the hotel arranged by Thomas Cook and continued the next day to Genoa. The train was warm and the express smooth, and best of all it was taking her from the ghastly cold and rain of Paris to her beloved Italy, where the climate was kinder and her sons would be waiting, plus the Blackers to talk about their education. Not that she was anxious to go to Germany, having only just settled at Sori with Otho and the Ranee. But Carlos was right about school in Heidelberg. Cyril was brooding over his father's offence, and school would take his mind off it. The Teutonic regime of German schools would suit her elder boy admirably, for he was athletic and well able to defend himself against all comers. Vivian, as his name was now spelt, was a more sensitive child. If she had any reservations about Germany, it was on this account.

Back in Sori, both Carlos Blacker and the Ranee persuaded her that a German education would toughen Vivian up, and she had to face the fact that for Oscar Wilde's children life was not going to be easy. And so she was won over to the idea. The Blackers invited her to stay with them until the boys were settled at whatever school she chose, so that if anything were to be discovered, she would be there to support them.

At this stage it must be said that the Blacker family provided the stability and comradeship which the Holland boys needed, and both they and their mother valued the friendship tremendously. Carlos's sons and nephews were their playfellows, and he became their trusted friend and adviser, writing to them at school and sending presents to celebrate their birthdays. He also took their mama out in his carriage in the Black Forest and on other scenic trips, for she could walk very little and otherwise would have not made the most of her visit. Mrs Blacker, whom Constance affectionately called 'Carrie', became her friend and, after leaving Freiburg, her correspondent. The women shared a common interest in photography, developing and enlarging their own films. Dr C. P. Blacker, their son, wrote of his father:

Carlos Blacker was born in 1859 and died in 1928. He was what used to be called a man of leisure, having no profession. He lived much abroad (Paris, Freiburg, Florence) and had a wide circle of friends including Bernard Shaw, Anatole France and J. G. Frazer, with whom he regularly corresponded. He was an exceptionally good linguist, speaking perfect French and Spanish and being fluent in many other languages. His memory was remarkable: he could recite most of Dante. . . . In his last years he taught himself Hebrew declaring that if he went to Heaven it would be useful to be able to speak to God in his own language! My father's main interests were literature, social anthropology and comparative religion. He was a wonderful conversationalist, and could draw people out making them feel cleverer than they really were. These gifts won him friends in all countries and in all stations in life. My brother (killed in the first war) and I used to ask him at the end of each day what new friends he had made and he would delight us, as children, by his accounts. His correspondence was enormous. It was in his letters and conversation (he published nothing) that he expressed himself. He had strong likes and dislikes. There were some people whom he refused to meet. But he involved himself emotionally in his friends' lives, being lifted up when they were successful or happy and cast down when they were in trouble. He was deeply distressed by the course of Wilde's life after his release from prison and used to try to cheer him up during the early part of his stay in Paris. (He also felt deeply for Constance Wilde with whom he corresponded.) My father tried to interest Wilde in the Dreyfus case by which he was much obsessed, being a close friend and confidant of Panizzardi. My father used to read aloud to us when we were children. One of my earliest recollections is of crying when he read me the 'Happy Prince' which Wilde had dedicated to my father.

Before embarking on the search for schools, the Ranee insisted that Constance see an eminent consultant in Genoa about her spinal injury, for she confessed to a fear that it was something other than a mere lumbar dislocation. Of all things she did not want to become an invalid. It was this fear that drove her to keep the appointment. The diagnosis did nothing to ease her fear. She was suffering from a kind of creeping paralysis, caused by pressure on the spine as a result of the fall down stairs. The only hope to stop the paralysis was an operation to relieve the pressure. In 1896 surgery, especially spinal surgery, was shrouded in mystery. The recovery rate was nowhere near that of today's standards, and the prospect of it must have filled her with dread. But it was either that or slowly losing the use of her limbs altogether. As the surgeon would have pointed out, she was only forty years old, still a beautiful woman and, once the pressure was relieved, would live out her allotted span. Early surgery was advisable, while she was still strong enough to bear it and make a more rapid recovery. She was emphatic in her refusal to enter the nursing home until the boys were settled, and once having set her mind to a thing, nothing could persuade her otherwise. Besides, the invigorating air at Heidelberg was bound to do her constitution good.

Before returning to her apartment she decided to be practical; handwriting was becoming difficult, and being an inveterate letter-writer, she invested some money in a typewriter on which to continue her correspondence unhampered. Having told the Ranee and Otho the results of the consultation, and outlining her determination to see the boys settled, Constance found herself once again on her travels.

Surrounded by portmanteaus, boxes and travelling rugs, she and boys set off on the first lap of the journey to the Blackers' residence in Freiburg.

It took some time to settle Cyril and Vivian. They had been at one school only three days when one of the masters set about beating Vivian over the head with rulers for some trivial offence; Cyril, always protective, came to his brothers' aid and kicked the master in the shins, followed by a punch in the stomach; then Vivian, seeing chance of retaliation, ran at the man and pitched him over.

After the expulsion, Constance entered them at another school, where they took exception to the anti-British attitude of the other twelve pupils, whom they challenged to fight it out—naturally they covered themselves in glory—as well as bloody noses—but the school authorities took a dim view of the escapade. The boys had been footloose and fancy free too long to settle down straight away. And Cyril, who was handy with his fists, was more likely to court disaster than run away from it. They lacked the influence of a father and a steady family background. The expulsions cannot have been without anxiety, for their mother lost no time at all in resuming her study of the brochures, wondering if the right school would ever be found. Finally, it began to dawn on her that schools with a Teutonic regime were not for the Holland boys, so she chose an English college called Neuenheim at which they were entered for the following term. Neuenheim was rather like a modern Dotheboys Hall in that most of the pupils were disadvantaged in some way, unwanted, exiled, difficult or suffering from parted parents. This suited the Holland children admirably, for, if most of the pupils had something to hide, they were less likely to pry into the affairs of others. The wheel had now turned full circle. Just as Oscar had seen the name of Sir William splashed across the newspaper placards in the Moll Travers affair, so Cyril, conscious of his father's criminal offence, was hugging to himself, with all the earnestness of his young years, the concealment not only of his own identity but of his brother's.

While the boys stayed with the Blackers' children during the long summer vacation, their mother took the opportunity to return to Italy for a few weeks to stay with the Ranee. The apartment at Sori had been relinquished, and Otho had returned, during the spring, to Bevaix.

Constance needed to discuss her affairs with the Ranee, for things had not been going well. While visiting her husband the previous year at Reading Gaol, they had arranged their legal and domestic affairs to the satisfaction of both, agreeing that after his release she and the boys would join him in France. Oscar had trusted her to arrange the marriage settlement, and indeed everything was arranged. But, as she feared, against Oscar's express wishes and instructions, which had been for her to buy Oscar's share, which was half, of the marriage settlement from the Official Receiver, his solicitor and friends had for some inexplicable reason interfered in the transaction. Consequently, her solicitor, Mr Hargrove, thought Oscar behind the move and, reverting to his old hostility, began to urge divorce again. She was worried because, if her husband heard she was going for divorce, which she was not, what would he think? How tortured he would be, thinking she had deserted him and that all her words at Reading had been pretence. While Constance was worrying about it all at Nervi, her husband, equally angry and frustrated, complained bitterly in a letter to Robbie Ross of both his own solicitor's handling of his affairs and the mismanagement of them by one of his advisers, More Adey. He likened him to a donkey, calling him dense and stupid and levelling accusations of the greatest incompetence. Then Robbie Ross's business acumen was called into account and found wanting. Both men had acted foolishly; it is only fair to say they were keen to get the best possible deal out of Constance's solicitors for their friend. The end result was totally against him both financially and on the domestic front.

Constance had always feared interference and felt as though she and Oscar were like pieces of a chessboard, being manoeuvred to the satisfaction of the players, namely his advisers and hers. She had given instructions that Oscar was not to be told of the serious nature of her back trouble; and yet again, she put off the necessary operation, this time because of Vivian. The regime at Neuenheim suited Cyril admirably but was too tough for the younger boy.

Princess Alice, having previously talked the matter over while visiting the Ranee, had entered Vivian at the Collegio della Visitazione in Monaco. It was a Jesuit college, which suited the boy's religious leanings, and the atmosphere was far more gentle and tolerant than that of Neuenheim. The Princess promised to keep an eye on Vivian and arranged with her favourite priest to allow him to spend his half holidays at the palace. Monaco was about six hours' travelling distance from Genoa, which was not too far for Constance to travel. Friends pointed out that it would make her life easier if she had both her sons boarded under one roof; but her paramount concern was for the school to suit their temperaments and that they should be happy.

Cyril was not so much happy at Neuenheim as safe from discovery. At thirteen he was making good progress and was familiar with the routine; in such a backwater of English education, among the expelled and deprived, his real identity would never now be discovered. His mother would not undermine his courage by moving him. When at Monaco, she and Vivian stayed at the Bristol Hotel; she showed her son about the town so that he would not feel at a disadvantage when out with the other boys, and of course cheered herself up by visiting the scintillating Alice. Her Serene Highness was quite incorrigible and not the least bit worried that her marriage was heading for the rocks and due to last only another two years before divorce closed in.

12

Fin de Siècle

As the time for Oscar's release drew nearer, fate was beginning to erect insuperable barriers about Constance, the permutations of which were overwhelming. With six months of his term left, she wondered how it would all end. He had been repentant and remorseful on her visit to Reading Gaol, but in view of the way things had turned out, had he been sincere? And when he was released, would they be able to discuss the future, face to face, or would this immense muddle have rendered understanding impossible? She worried about the operation and her health. Questions came painfully to mind. What if the operation was not a success? What if she and Oscar got together again and she became a permanent invalid? How would Oscar, with his natural abhorrence of the maimed, then regard his wife? And if he began to write again and became sought-after, as Otho maintained could very well happen, where would she figure in his new life? She would be useless to him, and knowing how he felt, would she be able to cope with his knowing, for no matter how devoted a show he put on, it would be playing a part. Of course he would not desert her after she had stood by him in prison, but how long before her role degenerated into a walking-on part? None of that was in her book. All the attendant emotional turmoil involved would kill her as surely as the disease.

While Constance had been settling her son at his new school, the Ranee had taken a small villa for her, near to her own at Bogliasco, just outside Genoa. The Ranee also engaged the sister of one of her own maids to run the place and look after Constance. The Villa Elvira was her first real home—not counting the shared apartment at Sori—since leaving the House Beautiful. Because she and Oscar were virtually estranged, through no fault of their own, she appreciated the security of the villa and its proximity to the Ranee.

In March, before Oscar was due to be released in May, his solicitors began to put on the pressure, urging her to a reconciliation with glowing pictures of how her influence would transform his life, while her own solicitors were wanting her to go ahead with divorce. Flailing about in the indecision which marked this period of her life, she took advice from Otho and discussed her situation with the Ranee. After all, the Ranee had survived her life in Borneo and, on being separated from the Rajah, had successfully brought up three sons, and lived for music and was wonderful and indominitable. Speranza had possessed the same spirit. Constance wished to be as strong and forceful and magnetic, but the burden of progressive ill health was slowly sapping her vitality and energy.

Oscar at this time genuinely appreciated all his wife had tried to do for him. Contrary to the opinion he had given his friends in the past, there was a self-confessed sincere affection in his heart for the woman he had chosen twelve years earlier to be the chatelaine of his dream house. With the threat of divorce once again looming over his head, he hoped Constance would remarry and find the peace and happiness which her brother had found in his second marriage, and which Willie also appeared to experience.

As for his children, Wilde was appalled to realize that he had forfeited every right to them and would be allowed to interfere only if he knew they were being neglected or uneducated—as if either were likely. At first he hoped the choice of a guardian would not be from his wife's family, for naturally they would present him in a bad light; he wished for one to bear the mark of neutrality, but in so delicate and intimate a situation it was not to be. At first he was disappointed when Adrian Hope, Laura's husband, filled the bill, but later on he admitted that the choice of Hope would ensure a secure future for Cyril and Vivian. Added to all this, the court declared him unfit to be with his own children, and, always a loving father—when he was at home, that is—this was the worst blow of all. His essential kindness of heart is shown by his not forgetting some children who were in prison for snaring rabbits; because he was being released, he could not bear for them to stay inside and asked the warder the amount of their fine, which he paid for their release.

A Deed of Arrangement seemed to have placed everything outside the control of both Wilde and his wife. The finances were that Oscar was to receive an allowance of £150 a year from his wife's estate, and if she died before him it was to be paid for as long as he lived. This was on condition he did nothing which would "entitle his wife to a divorce or a decree for judicial separation, or be guilty of any moral misconduct or notoriously consort with evil or disreptable companions". At this stage Adrian Hope stated that he was now practically the sole adviser of Constance Wilde, both in her own interests and in those of the children, and that it was immaterial to him what kind of life Wilde led out of prison, provided "he did not molest his wife and provided he kept out of the newspapers". In the event of any further public scandal, Adrian would apply at once for authority to stop the allowance. It was also impressed upon the prisoner "how absolutely fatal to him any further intercourse with Lord Alfred Douglas will be". Clearly the panic which Wilde's release engendered almost matched that of his incarceration!

Although the subject of the divorce was once again shelved, Sidney Hargrove insisted Constance allow a trial period to elapse before she and Oscar saw each other. As the time of his release drew ever nearer, she could not make up her mind entirely about her husband. There was still a little of the rebel in her personality, a desire in defiance of all to go to the man who had always fascinated her. But now there was hesitation and indecision; time, for her, had lessened the depravity of the criminal offence for which he had been severely punished; time, distance, separation and exile had all contributed to blur the edges of reality. But her family could not forgive or forget, and people in London would always retain an interest, an avid interest, in the name of Wilde. If there had been no children, she would have had no hesitation in going to join Oscar, but, knowing him as she did, she needed further proof of his sincerity before subjecting the children to further turmoil. Compare Constance's attitude of mind at this time with the firm, no-nonsense approach at any hint of censure about her engagement. If her illness had not been taking its toll, the Oscar Wilde story might have been different. This quixotic aspect now emerging in her character shows itself in the following incident.

On 17th May 1897, after serving two years' hard labour, Wilde was about to be released from prison. First he had to sign the Deed of Arrangement, a copy of which had been sent out to Italy for Constance's signature. And although it was neither necessary nor indeed desirable, Constance, against medical advice, had travelled from Italy to put in a personal but heavily veiled appearance. Wilde's solicitor, in whose company she was, must have wondered what there was in this bedevilled relationship to bring Mrs Wilde on such an errand. On her arrival in London the interest of the Press in her husband's release would not have escaped her, and the anticipatory announcement splashed across the hoardings, "Release of Oscar Wilde", would be a chilling reminder of the vituperation once aroused.

The warder who was on duty at Reading Gaol, "in sight but out of hearing", for the purpose of the visit, said that Mrs Wilde accompanied the solicitor but did not wish the prisoner to see her. Oscar sat at a table with his head in his hands, opposite the lawyer. His appearance at the time was reported by a newspaper man as "looking very well. His build and general appearance were—as of old—distinguished and attractive. In short the Oscar Wilde of today is the Oscar Wilde." Actually, he was thinner and looked older, and his hair was greying at the temples. Outside in the passage Constance waited, a slender figure, poised and fashionably dressed in black. While the consultation was in progress, she turned to the warder and asked a favour of him. "Let me have one glimpse of my husband?" she asked. He moved aside respectfully to enable her to look through the glass peep-hole in the door. The Deed of Arrangement was lying on the table, and at that precise moment Wilde was in the act of appending his signature to the document and signing away any right to see his children without their mother's consent. In the warder's words, "Mrs Wilde cast one long lingering glance inside, and saw the convict-poet, who, in deep mental distress himself, was totally unconscious that any eyes save those of the stern lawyer and myself witnessed his degradation." Seeing him sign the deed, she drew back, "apparently labouring under deep emotion", and a few minutes later she left the prison with the solicitor. To the warder it remained "the saddest story" he knew of the prisoner.

Why, one wonders, did Constance travel so far and yet not meet with him? Was she by now intimidated in a way and afraid to go beyond the advice of Adrian Hope and Sidney Hargrove? If they had known of the visit, surely she would have been in Hargrove's company and not that of her husband's solicitor? Was the relationship between them too strained to withstand a confrontation, or were the emotional circumstances too fragile? Whatever her reason, she shared what was possibly the most distressing moment in both their lives. An additional twist of the knife in her heart would have been his improved looks. His face had lost its coarseness and in appearance would have been as she had known it in the early days, the happy days—and as he looked again only after death.

And what of her after she left Reading? She probably stayed in her safe retreat with Miss Boxwell in her top-floor apartment at Holbein House until after Oscar's discharge. She was certainly not aware of the plans for this; no one, not even Oscar, knew exactly what was to happen. The prison authorities engaged in some cloak-and-dagger activities to ensure that the 'poet-convict' was restored to the world with as little fuss as possible. Firstly he was transferred by cab and train to Pentonville, where he was received by the Governor and where none of the officers were even aware of the prisoner's name. Next morning, Wednesday 17th May, "A private conveyance containing two gentlemen arrived at 6.10 a.m. It was admitted to the courtyard and turned round, the prisoner then got into it and was driven off totally unobserved by anyone. Inquiries were made by strangers soon after 6.30 who continued to watch the prison until after the normal discharges left." He was then taken to the house of the Reverend Stewart Headlam in Upper Bedford Place, to change and take breakfast. Soon Ernest and Ada Leverson arrived, followed by other friends, to celebrate his release. Later in the day, accompanied by More Adey, he dodged newspaper men and, to avoid recognition at Victoria Station, took a cab to West Croydon on the first leg of his journey into exile. They then took the ferry from Newhaven to Dieppe. Possibly, at the same time Constance would be travelling back to her villa, wondering if this was the end—or the beginning.

Unfortunately Oscar's stay in Dieppe was brevity itself, for, as the proprietor of the Hotel Glion had asked Constance to move on some two years before, so did the proprietors of the cafés and restaurants at Dieppe—at the request of their English clientele. A letter from the preserver of the town's morals—if it ever had any—warned Oscar that in the event of any "irregularities of conduct" he would be drummed not only out of town but out of the country. Clearly, this was not the place for peace of mind. Oscar then moved on a few miles to Berneval sur Mer, a small village about ten miles north-east of Dieppe, where, presumably, the English were either thin on the ground or of a more tolerant nature.

Adopting the name of Sebastian Melmoth, he settled at Berneval, where he enjoyed swimming in the sea and attended Mass. Totally submerged in the first joys of freedom, he could not yet envisage anything further; but one thing was certain: if he wanted to see Cyril and Vivian again, there was only one path to take, and he must tread it alone until the solicitors considered that a decent interval had elapsed.

Constance wrote to her husband every week, and he was pleased with a photograph of her which Robbie Ross had sent. She obviously did not realize that a regular correspondence of a friendly nature would raise Oscar's hopes of being united with his family. He was anxious to see her and the boys, and it was only a matter of weeks before he was suggesting a meeting.

"There he is in Berneval," sympathetic friends told her, "not Oscar Wilde but Sebastian Melmoth; no home, no family, no one to care for him." Yet Constance, because of fear of her advisers, dithered. Others suggested she go and take him in hand, before someone else did—meaning, of course, Alfred Douglas. But the state of her marriage before the advent of Alfred Douglas was hardly encouragement to begin again. Was there any foundation left on which to rebuild? And what if she flouted the advice of Mr Hargrove, and they returned to Oscar as a family? What if, as before, they were not enough for him? Where would she be then? Her life would be a series of 'I told you so.' It would be intolerable for her, and immensely cruel for the boys, if reunited they were deserted again, especially since Cyril had made such a cult of 'being a man'. Then her other self would argue that, once Oscar beheld his sons and became the object of their love and admiration, he would not go off again. In reality, it was not so much Oscar's being a failure that she was afraid of as herself.

Meanwhile Carlos Blacker, nice man that he was, trotted back and forth in person and letter, between her and Oscar, bearing messages like a "bookie's runner", as the Ranee said. In order to put off the impending meeting, Carlos was given leave to inform Oscar that Constance's illness was progressively worsening. He had not realized the magnitude of it and was genuinely shocked; he came up with the bright idea, however, of going to see her instead of her coming to see him. Let's meet and get it over with, was his philosophy, but Carlos advised against it and suggested he defer any action until September.

Oscar, reading between the lines—and rightly so, construed this to mean when the boys had returned to their schools. During the long summer vacation when her sons were at the Villa Elvira, Constance was on tenterhooks lest they discover anything about their father, especially Cyril. Oscar had sent her a copy of the *Daily Chronicle* in which he had written a tremendous article asking for a full Home Office enquiry into the cruelty to children in prisons. It was in her mind to show it to Cyril, pointing out that he had read of his father's disgrace on a newspaper hoarding and now he could read of his father's redemption through the article, but she could not bring herself to do it and in the end burned the paper. Oscar, meanwhile had started on his last work, the poem *The Ballad of Reading Gaol*.

Constance felt small, and mean and petty but because of her illness was willing to go along with indecision; having grown so used to the waiting, to her advisers acting on her behalf, she, like Oscar, was becoming something of a fatalist.

Before the boys returned to school, she took them in to Genoa to have their photographs taken. They looked smart and scrubbed and wore Eton collars. She sent the photographs to their father along with a note from each of the boys.

Perhaps the gesture was not as altruistic as it sounds, but a kind of sop to her conscience for not allowing him the access. At such times her mind was off again on the merry-go-round of what Carlos said, what the Ranee said, what Mr Hargrove said, what Adrian Hope said, what they all said! But with the children out of the way, she had more time for panic-less consideration. It seemed that, as she was going to be involved in some degree with her husband during the next few months, why not, as Oscar had said, see him and get it over with? To be living in continuous doubt as to what they really thought of each other seemed absurd. She was haunted also by the existence of Alfred Douglas, the devil which could not be exorcized. He was still about, a pale, golden, aristocratic figure, hovering in the wings. A rival *par excellence*. Straight-limbed and young, a poet—there was nothing withered about Alfred. And how she hated him.

Cyril and Vivian being back at school, there was nothing to stop her communicating directly with her husband. In a flurry of exhilarating euphoria, and in the same frame of mind as she had been in at Glion when she had instructed her brother to write the clandestine letter, she laboriously typed and signed the note addressed to 'Sebastian Melmoth' in Berneval. It was despatched with an air of well-being and satisfaction. If not hurried and chivvied, she could solve her own affairs. Something positive had been done at last—no matter what they said, she was doing what she desired. As for the consequences of her action—she awaited their development with intense anticipation.

It was not unusual for letters to take a week between Dieppe and Genoa, but when two weeks had passed and there was still no reply from Oscar, the anticipation turned to apprehension. Why had he not replied? Perhaps he had not received the letter—worse, what if, receiving it, he did not, after her previous refusals, want to see her now? Suspense was lengthened on hearing from a mutual friend who had been in Dieppe that Oscar was greatly distressed and supposed he should never see his children again. He told the mutual friend that life had suddenly turned black and suicidal.

A further week passed. Strained, apprehensive and remorseful, she waited. At last Carlos Blacker brought a devastating reply. Her husband, who had been depressed, lonely and worn out with her perpetual procrastinations, was going to buy a villa in Naples—with Alfred Douglas. Bosie, he told their friend, had offered him a home.

Constance realized she had dallied too long and left her willingness to see Oscar too late. Douglas had got there first. Oscar knew that his reference to a home would mean something to her, for he had said often, on returning to Tite Street, "I pity with all my heart those poor creatures who have no home." Was it her fault that he had no home? Of course it was not, she would tell herself. How could he, how dare he, she would enquire indignantly, refer to three months of perpetual procrastination! What was a mere three months compared with the terrible two years she had had to go through? His weakness appalled her. And the enormity of his folly aroused her temper. Had he really gone to Naples to see about a villa with Alfred Douglas, she wondered, or was it a statement intended to spur her to some kind of action?

She immediately wrote a furious note demanding to know the truth of the matter. She also cast aspersions on his alleged concern for his sons. He had not even bothered to acknowledge the little letters they had sent with the photographs. One wonders why he did not do this. Did he think Constance would not have passed them on? And, indeed, in the nervous state she was now in, would she?

Once again the days crept by, measured not in minutes and hours but by the calls of the village postmaster. Her friends in Nervi remarked: "What a lucky escape you've had. Just think, if you had joined up and then this had happened, oh, my dear!" Some averred that leopards never changed their spots, and Carlos pointed out the wisdom of a probationary period. But all Constance could see, in the absence of a letter, was Alfred Douglas, Lucifer personified. And when it became obvious that there would be no letter denying Oscar's going to Naples with Alfred, flames of anger and jealousy began to build up. She re-lived, in a lurid light, the implications of their relationship. The horror of the trials. The changing of their name. Cyril's young life already spoilt beyond redemption. She felt the weight keenly—of what? Remorse? Jealousy? Resentment? Ever a one to feel resentment when totally depressed, it seemed that all past resentments flooded over her, building up in a wave of truculence on whose crest she poised herself to observe, as though someone else, her husband's pathetic weakness. He had let her down in more ways than one. She had trusted him. Mr Hargrove and Adrian Hope and Laura would be nodding their heads and lifting up their hands in gestures of 'what else could she expect?' The siren calls of Alfred must have been strong because, in going back to him, Oscar knew he would forfeit his allowance. It was part of the agreement he had signed before leaving prison. How idiotic of her to have thought that she and Oscar could ever have lived together again! Nothing now could ever be as before. What had happened now—no matter whose fault it was—had happened for ever. She could not, after this second betrayal, ever accept Oscar back into her life. Disillusionment was now complete. Dry-eyed, rigid with rage and contempt and stung by his silence into fury, she sent him a scathing letter referring to Alfred Douglas in terms of indescribable loathing, and in which she wielded her legal prerogative of forbidding him to come and see her. The renewal of Oscar's friendship with Douglas—moreover a public renewal—did nothing for either her sensitivity or her constitution. Her illness was worsening, and the fearful anxiety was bound to pull her down. But worse news was to come: the Marquess of Queensberry had engaged private detectives to track his son down. The return to Douglas was an appalling blow to Constance's ego; she was a proud woman and never recovered from it.

By November she had given up tormenting herself as to what Douglas and her husband were doing at Naples . . . visions of them holding hands . . . seated together . . . Oscar, as she had seen before, beguiled beyond measure, smiling down at Bosie, his arm extended about the young man's neck. Were they comforting each other? Were they discussing her letter—or, worse, discussing her! Oh, the special, the absolute cruelty. But it was passing.

Constance's letter was followed by a more terrible one still, from Bosie's mother, Lady Queensberry. Their sharing of a villa in Naples had been reported in the English newspapers, and her ladyship had followed Constance's example by stopping her son's allowance. When their money ran out, she hoped it would be followed by her son.

Constance's paralysis meanwhile was encroaching, and the thought must have crossed her mind more than once whether, as with her decision about Oscar, she had dallied too long. But Christmas would bring the boys from their schools, and there was comfort in anticipation; also, there would be recollection. Last Christmas she had hoped that her husband's release would work some kind of magic, some easing of a frustrating situation. But the magic had not worked, and this second betrayal had invested her life with a bitterness, a melancholy, with which she scarcely knew how to cope.

Her choice of literature at this particular time is indicative of her frame of mind. There was, in November that year, a parcel of books despatched from Hatchard's in Piccadilly to the Villa Elvira. It contained three books obviously for the boys, for which she had sent payment. The other was a gift of her own choice from the manager, Arthur Humphries, who had seen to the publication of *Oscariana* some three years since and with whom she had attended Pre-Raphaelite meetings. He found her "a charming lady, and a lively correspondent". Her choice was not every woman's idea of Christmas reading, but it was strangely apposite, for she had asked for Epictetus. He was a Greek philosopher who, to put it briefly, stresses the power of the mind to rise above worldly misfortunes and ills, distinguishing clearly between the things that are in our power and control and those that are not. This philosophy is not so much academic as a means of comfort and an aid to living.

Even her Christmas hopes were blighted, in that she was denied the pleasure of having her sons home together. Vivian, being at a religious college, was expected to take part in the Masses and Vigils attendant upon the season, so his mother wrote and promised she would go to Monaco in the New Year and that they would spend a whole week together. Cyril travelled from Neuenheim alone. Overflowing with high spirits, health and energy, the sight of him was enough to make her feel better.

The admittance to the nursing home was further delayed on account of the promised week with Vivian. The snows lingered over the mountains until well into the new year of 1898, making travelling, even along the coastal road, subject to delays. Not wanting to combat any uncertainties in her present state of health, Constance waited until February before making the promised journey to visit her younger son.

The warmth and mildness of the early spring in Monaco, and the sight of the palm trees, melted away the chill of melancholy thoughts, making them as remote as the snow on the high passes. With an upsurge of the true spirit of aestheticism, she gave herself up entirely to the sensation of the whole week with Vivian. Having received permission to take him from the college, she booked rooms at the Bristol Hotel and whisked him off as though it were a high-spirited prank. And yet he was a poignant reminder of the husband she was trying to forget. Vivian was a Wilde, sensitive, emotional and highly appreciative of the finer things in life. His young face reflected his father's. The long jawline, full lips, straight hair which flopped onto his forehead, and slanting, almost almond-shaped eyes. Dressed in college uniform and, as is usually the case with small boys, he looked so engagingly vulnerable that his mother decided the week was to be his alone, to do whatever he wanted.

A visit to take tea with Princess Alice could hardly have been the eleven-year-old's idea, for Vivian preferred to take his tea with the children of visiting relatives in the nursery and afterwards hunt for stamps. No doubt Oscar's return to Bosie Douglas, and their Serene Highnesses' extra-marital affairs, formed the basis of a 'good old gossip' between the women.

Meanwhile Oscar, back in Naples, was waxing indignant about the loss of his allowance. His solicitor had apparently pointed out to him that he could not possibly expect his wife to give him money to subsidize his relationship with Douglas, but the logic of this reasoning escaped him.

When Constance arrived back at her villa, she was greatly relieved to hear that Alfred and Oscar had agreed to part company; it was really more of a prising apart for monetary reasons. The pair were broke, hard-up and had not a penny between them. The reason was that Oscar had ran out of money, and Lady Queensberry had followed Constance's example by stopping Alfred's allowance. Her ladyship offered further inducement to the impoverished Wilde in the form of

£200—on condition that he did not see her son again, and he never did. The money was paid to Oscar via Robbie Ross, who doled it out in small amounts, for Oscar, always extravagant—and more so now Alfred had gone—was drinking more than was good for him and would have spent it all in a very short time.

Another piece of good news was that Oscar had written a long poem about his prison experience and called it *The Ballad of Reading Gaol*. It had been published in February by that shady yet intriguing character Leonard Smithers. Among those to whom Wilde asked his publisher to send complimentary copies were Constance and her brother, who wrote his appreciation of it. Constance, in spite of her husband's behaviour, thought it a beautiful piece of work, a jewel wrought from all the horror; she wept because he was so gifted and his life so frightfully tragic.

Eventually there were letters from Oscar to his wife seeking to renew his allowance, but, of course, this was in the hands of the lawyers. She had no control over it—Oscar had signed his own fate. So persistent were these requests that she began to be afraid of being hounded for money for the rest of her life. After all, she had her home to maintain and the boys to bring up and educate. And there was always the danger that, if she did not answer the letters, he might one day turn up on her doorstep! Moreover, he complained to their friends about her, which she resented bitterly, for, being herself in touch with Robbie Ross, she sent small amounts for Robbie to disburse. Although not wanting to see or to write to Oscar, she did not want him to starve. When Carlos Blacker was going to Paris on business, she asked him to go and see her husband, hoping the conversation would provide the necessary shot in the arm to get Oscar writing again while the *Ballad* was still in the public eye. It did not work out that way. Carlos ended up lending Wilde some money, ostensibly for the hotel bill! Eventually, she offered to send 10 francs a day for his lodging at a shabby little hotel on the rue des Beaux Arts, the Hôtel d'Alsace—to the hotel-keeper, of course, which meant that at least Oscar had a roof over his head and the basic necessities of life.

On 24th March, a week or so before she was, at last, being admitted to the nursing home, she opened her English copy of the *Daily Chronicle* to see a long letter headed, 'Don't Read This If You Want To Be Happy Today.' Public opinion was still so sensitive that the letter did not bear Wilde's name but rather the words, 'Author of the Ballad of Reading Gaol'. The second reading of the Prison Bill was being debated in the House of Commons that week, and Wilde set before the public in general and the House in particular a number of suggestions for prison reform. Some of the recommendations were actually implemented and became part of the Prison Act. Many of his friends urged him to gather material for a book on the subject, but after making a half-hearted attempt he gave up the idea. In the letter he was still tilting, like Don Quixote, at society, and the last paragraph must have raised a little smile. "But to make these reforms effectual," he wrote, "much has to be done, and the first and perhaps the most difficult task is to humanise the governors of the prisons, to civilise the warders and to Christianize the chaplains." She was also to read, though with not as much pleasure, in the society columns of a French newspaper that Lord Alfred Douglas, unlike Oscar, was not shunned by respectable society but was reported to have attended functions held at the British Embassy at Rome.

Undergoing operations or entering hospital often provides the stimulus for drawing up or altering wills, setting one's affairs in order, and Constance, especially with her complicated domestic and monetary problems, was no exception. She knew that after her death her husband, who was by now quite reckless about money, would receive short shrift at the hands of Adrian Hope and Sidney Hargrove. So she left instructions that after her death his original allowance should be restored. The day before the operation she sent him a nice letter and £40 to Robbie Ross to disburse to her husband as necessary. She also wrote a long letter to each of her sons.

At last the operation to relieve the pressure on her spine, which was by this time reported to be the cause of unbearable pain, was to take place. Constance had a sense of everything being now in order, and death, if it came, would bring release from being interminably and inextricably bound to the man she had married. Unable to cast him off and forget about him, it was almost a case of not being able to live with him and not being able to live without him. Death, if it came, would do justice to her own dignity, for there could be nothing now from a relationship with Oscar but bouts of Holland temper on her part and sponging letters on his. It was impossible to remake the past. She and Oscar had modelled their own destinies and of necessity now had become vague and misted figures, overlaid with misunderstandings and misrepresentation.

Constance never recovered from the operation; perhaps she had left it too late and the paralysis was too far advanced; perhaps she had been weakened physically and emotionally—even mentally—by the long-drawn-out troubles which surrounded her. There are signs of her running away to hide, as it were, inside herself, retreating from an unpleasant world. Both Otho Holland and the Ranee told Vyvyan later on in his life that his mother had no suspicion of death, but, judging by her last letter to him, he could only think that she had. The arrangements which she made bear this out, and the constant use of the phrase "after my death" and not, as one might say, "in the event of my death".

She died on 7th April 1898, aged forty, and had retained her good looks despite all her suffering and troubles.

There is a rather bizarre report surrounding her demise that comes from Alfred Douglas, who heard it from Harry de Windt, the Ranee's brother. He stated that Mrs Wilde went to Genoa on private business and did not return to her villa. It was some days later when the Ranee was notified of her death, which had taken place at a hotel in Genoa. Yet another version is that she went for a drive while convalescent from the operation, collapsed and was taken to a hotel where she died of a seizure. The exact date of any operation is not clear. She was still at Bogliasco on 30th March, for she wrote an extremely cheerful letter to Carlos Blacker from the Villa Elvira—and eight days later she was dead. In the letter there was no mention of the operation or comment on her health; on the contrary, she was making plans and looking ahead. It could be, of course, that having had the operation she was returning to the villa to recuperate and the journey proved too much. Whatever the circumstances, her death took place on 7th April.

Otho broke the news to Oscar by way of telegram and afterwards made all the funeral arrangements. He also telegraphed the sad news to England. Laura Hope's journal contained the following entry: "April 8th. 1898. A telegram from Genoa with the news of poor Constance Wilde's death—asking Adrian to break it to the Napiers—so we went there after lunch and sad it was for they loved her dearly. Then we walked across Kensington Gardens and saw the lawyer, for Adrian is trustee and executor—so this means much business."

Neither Oscar, Vyvyan nor Cyril attended the funeral service. It was a simple affair; there was none of the pomp and ceremony which had surrounded her grandfather's funeral, or the glowing tributes which had followed her father to his grave. The committal took place in the Protestant part of the magnificent cemetery of Staglieno.

The sudden and unexpected news caused Oscar great grief. He

wished they had met, if only once, and kissed each other. However, by Maytime he was in receipt of his allowance again, as Constance had requested in her Will, and feeling piqued that his solicitor had consulted Adrian Hope about it—unnecessarily, he thought. The following year he made a visit to where his wife was buried. He was very moved as he stood by the marble cross, for her married name had been omitted by the family so that "she might not take her disgrace to the grave." It bore merely her Christian names, "Constance Mary, daughter of Horace Lloyd Q.C.", and a verse from the book of Revelations. Oscar abandoned himself to a moment of passionate grief, and, as he laid red roses upon the grave, he broke down and sobbed bitterly in an anguish of sorrow and regret.

A couple of years later, Wilde, too, was dead. He died on 30th November 1900 of cerebral meningitis; he was forty-six. A plain tombstone was erected over his grave at Bagneaux Cemetery, but in 1909 his remains were transferred to the French National Cemetery of Père Lachaise.

The Staglieno enjoys an equivalent status—being to Genoa what Père Lachaise is to Paris. Situated in the foothills above the valley of Bisagno, it is made up of imposing monuments which illustrate the style of Ligurian art and symbolize the spirit of romance which Constance so much loved. Just as Oscar in death at last received recognition, so Constance is not forgotten either. In the official guide to the Staglieno, all the noteworthy names are writ large in bold print, and among the Schmidt-Moston family and the Whiteread-Morigon-Bentley family is the name of Oscar Wilde's wife. And so the dishonoured name which her family at the end of the nineteenth century tried to conceal is now, in a more enlightened age, mentioned with pride—a fitting tribute to a heroine of the *fin de siècle*.

Bibliography

Birnbaum, Martin, *Oscar Wilde, Fragments and Memories*, 1920
Blunt, Wilfred Scawen, *My Diaries*, 1921
Bremont, Comtesse de, *Oscar Wilde and his Mother*, 1911
Brasil, Boris, *Oscar Wilde*, 1938
Croft-Cooke, Rupert, *Bosie*, 1963
Douglas, Lord Alfred, *Autobiography*, 1929
Gaunt, William, *Aesthetic Adventure*, 1945
Hart-Davis, Rupert, *Letters of Oscar Wilde*, 1962
Hichens, Robert, *Green Carnation*, 1894
Holland, Vyvyan, *Son of Oscar Wilde*, 1954
Hope-Nicholson, Jaqueline, *Life Among the Troubridges*, 1968
Hyde, H. Montgomery, *Trials of Oscar Wilde*, 1948
Hyde, H. Montgomery, *Aftermath*, 1963
Hyde, H. Montgomery, *Cases that Changed the Law*, 1951
Irvine, W. F., *Lancashire Hollands*, 1902
Jullian, Philippe, *Oscar Wilde*, 1971
Ladies' Pictorial, 1887
Langtry, Lillie, *The Days I knew*, 1925
Leverson, Ada, *Letters to the Sphinx*, 1930
Payne, Robert, *White Rajah of Sarawak*, 1960

Queensbury and Colson, *Oscar Wilde and the Black Douglas*, 1949
Quennell, Peter, *Ruskin*, 1949
Raffalovich, André, *Letters*, 1884
Rodd, Sir Rennell, *Social and Diplomatic Memories*, 1922
Rothenstein, William, *Men and Memories*, Vol. 1, 1931
Sherard, Robert, *Life of Oscar Wilde*, 1906
Sherard, Robert, *The Real Oscar Wilde*, 1911
Sherard, Robert, *The Story of an Unhappy Friendship*, 1902
Symonds, J., *Madam Blavatsky*, 1959
Westminster Chess Club Papers, May 1, 1874
White, Terence de Vere, *Parents of Oscar Wilde*, 1967
Women's World, 1888/9
Wratislaw, Theodore, *A Memoir*, 1979
Wyndham, Horace, *The Sphinx and Her Circle*, 1963

Index